YOU CAN CODE

MAKE YOUR OWN GAMES, APPS AND MORE

IN SCRATCH AND PYTHON!

Suitable for **COMPLETE BEGINNERS**

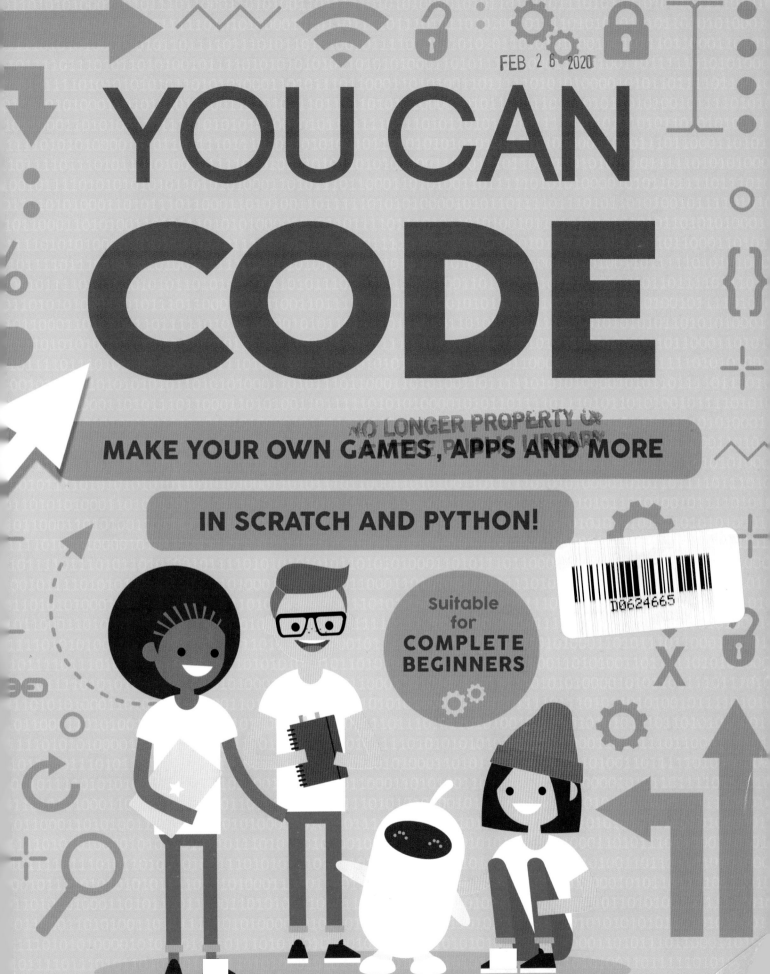

THIS IS A CARLTON BOOK

Published in 2019 by Carlton Books Limited, an imprint of the Carlton Publishing Group,
20 Mortimer Street, London W1T 3JW

The publishers would like to thank the following sources for their kind permission to reproduce
the pictures in this book.
Nadia Snopek/Shutterstock
Shutterstock: bioraven, Cookie Studio, Idea store, N.MacTavish, miniwide, Nadya_Art, Natali
Snailcat, openeyed, PremiumArt, Quarta, Rvector, siridhata, Sketch Master, VectorShow
Wikimedia Commons

Every effort has been made to acknowledge correctly and contact the source and/or copyright
holder of each picture and Carlton Books Limited apologises for any unintentional errors of
omissions, which will be corrected in future editions of this book.

A catalogue record for this book is available from the British Library.

ISBN: 978 1 78312 483 1

Printed in Dubai

10 9 8 7 6 5 4 3 2 1

Designed and packaged by: Dynamo Limited
Written by: Kevin Pettman
Managing Art Editor: Matt Drew
Editorial Manager: Joff Brown
Production: Nicola Davey

YOU CAN CODE

MAKE YOUR OWN GAMES, APPS AND MORE IN SCRATCH AND PYTHON!

CARLTON BOOKS

CONTENTS

WHAT IS CODING?

Coding is a set of instructions that computers follow. A computer can't create the code, so it must be written by a human. Another word for coding is programming. A programmer gives instructions to a computer.

The instructions a programmer gives a computer must be easy to follow and **give the machine a step-by-step guide**. Imagine if a programmer got the code wrong for a games controller and the 'left' button took your character to the right and the 'right' button went left! Each part of the code must be correct so it all works properly.

HOW MANY TIMES DO YOU USE COMPUTERS EACH DAY?

Working on a laptop at school... playing console games at home... watching videos on a tablet... sending messages with a mobile... you use computers more than you think. Everyday things like electronic toys, washing machines, watches, traffic lights and supermarket checkout scanners **all use computers too**!

Code may look complicated, but each part of the code must be a simple order for the computer to understand.

CRACK THE CODE

- - - - - - - - -

The English mathematician Ada Lovelace was **the world's first programmer**. In 1842 she explained how simple cards with punched holes in them could be used by a calculating machine.

But don't worry - there's **no need to be a computer genius**! This awesome guidebook takes you through the basics and shows you **how to create easy and fun code**. You'll set up games and add sounds, special effects, animations, music and much more amazing stuff.

▶ **SO, CAN YOU CODE? OF COURSE YOU CAN!**

SCRATCH

One of the easiest coding languages is Scratch, so it's a great place to start your coding journey. Most of this book uses Scratch to create fun and fascinating projects on your screen.

This awesome guide makes Scratch fun and easy to follow!

WORLDWIDE WOW

Scratch has **over 35 million users** in more than 150 countries and 40 languages. It was first released for general use in 2007.

5 SCRATCH FACTS

1 Scratch is **simple but clever**. Instead of having to type letters, numbers and symbols, the programmer (you!) just clicks and drags coloured blocks into place.

2 Scratch is **free**! That means millions of users can spend hours playing, building and saving projects and never pay a penny.

3 It was created by the **brilliant people** at the Massachusetts Institute of Technology (MIT) Media Lab in the USA.

4 Scratch games often begin with the programmer placing people or objects onto their screen. These are called **sprites**.

5 Scratch lets you **share** the coded projects you make with the Scratch community. You can 'remix' projects by others by copying and adding new bits. Scratch also lets you follow your favourite programmers, known as **Scratchers**.

 python

Another coding language, Python, appears from page 58. Python uses text and not blocks but is still an **easy coding system** to understand. You're now ready to launch into the Scratch scene, so turn over to start your **epic adventure**!

Why stop at Scratch? Check out Python!

SETTING UP SCRATCH

The Scratch website is scratch.mit.edu. Scratch can be played using an internet connection to this website. This is called being 'online'. It can also be used 'offline', which means you need an internet connection to download it to your computer or tablet first so it can then be used in the future without needing the internet.

ONLINE

At the Scratch homepage, click the mouse arrow on the words 'Join Scratch' at the top. Think of **your own Scratch username** and a password you can remember (ask an adult to help if you need to). When that's complete, click 'Create' to begin a Scratch project.

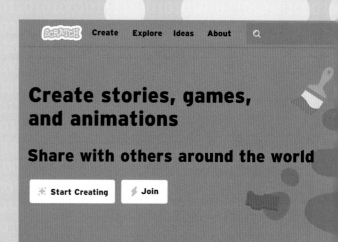

Create stories, games, and animations

Share with others around the world

✦ Start Creating   ⚡ Join

WWW.SCRATCH.MIT.EDU

USERNAME:

PASSWORD:

PERMISSION TO PLAY

Always check with your parent, guardian or the owner of the computer if it's okay to use Scratch.

OFFLINE

After joining Scratch, click on 'Offline Editor' at the bottom to install Scratch Desktop so that Scratch can be opened from your computer's applications.

The instructions in this book are for Scratch 3.0, the version of Scratch launched in January 2019. The older Scratch 2.0 and Scratch 1.4 versions are a bit different.

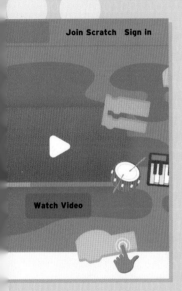

Scratch is named after scratching, a technique rappers and DJs use to remix music. The Scratch programming language lets you copy other people's projects and remix them to make your own versions.

Your younger brother or sister might like to try ScratchJr... but maybe not if they're still a baby!

YOUNG USERS

Scratch is designed for youngsters aged between eight and 16, but it can be used by anyone. Younger children might like to try the simple ScratchJr app at **www.scratchjr.org**

SCRATCH SCREEN GUIDE

After clicking on 'Create', your screen will look like this. It's called the interface, and it's where your coding projects happen.

TUTORIALS

Tutorials have helpful and simple videos showing how to code and build.

CODE TAB

Clicking on the 'Code' tab means you can see the blocks palette. The different coloured circles, such as **motion** and **looks**, takes you to that group of blocks.

BLOCKS PALETTE

On the left side of the interface, this is where you drag coding blocks from.

BACKPACK

Found at the bottom of the interface, this area is used to store sprites, sounds and scripts. Click and drag them here, then they can easily be dropped into other programs. If backpack isn't open, **click on the word** and it will expand.

EXTENSIONS

From the extensions library you add **new block sets**, such as music, LEGO and many more.

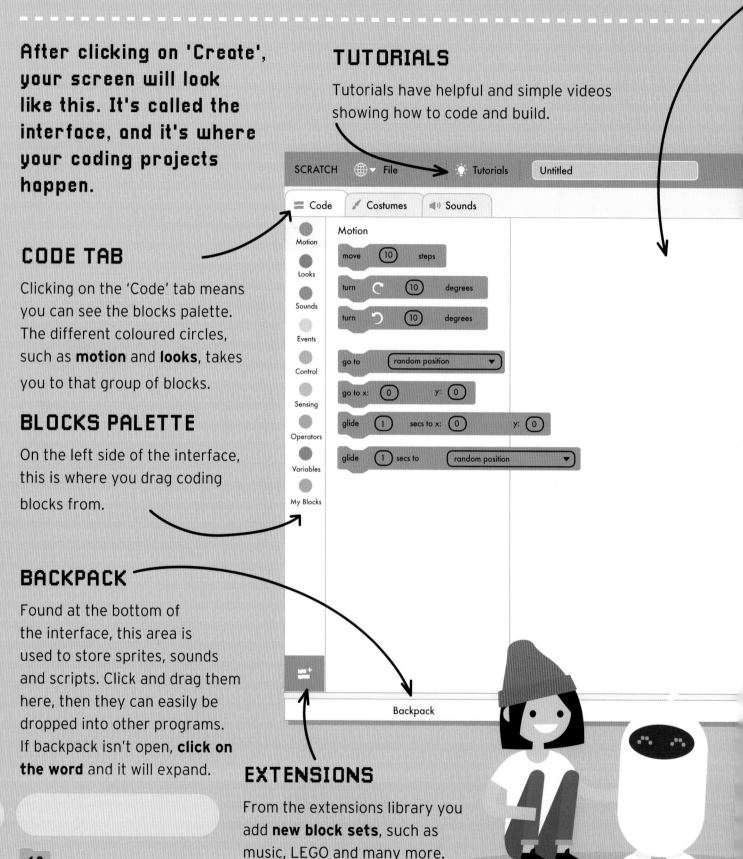

SCRIPTING AREA

In the centre of your screen. The script area is where you place blocks together to build a script, which is your **set of instructions**.

Click the green flag to start (run) a program and the red button to stop it.

STAGE AREA

Found in the top right of the interface. This is where sprites, backdrop images and sounds are added and where your coded games and creations **come to life**.

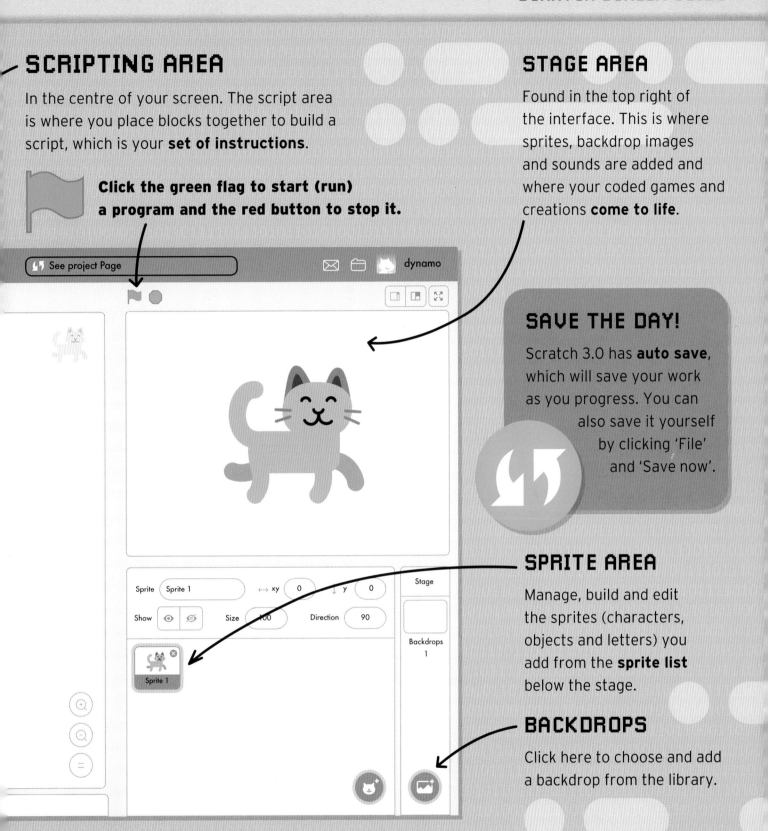

SAVE THE DAY!

Scratch 3.0 has **auto save**, which will save your work as you progress. You can also save it yourself by clicking 'File' and 'Save now'.

SPRITE AREA

Manage, build and edit the sprites (characters, objects and letters) you add from the **sprite list** below the stage.

BACKDROPS

Click here to choose and add a backdrop from the library.

There are lots more fun functions and cool stuff that Scratch will let you do, but these are the basic bits to get you started!

SPOTLIGHT ON SPRITES

Hey, look what I can do!

Oh wow!

Sprites are the most important part of Scratch and the sprite area is where you'll start to create your first simple project. By building a script to instruct them, sprites can be made to move, make sounds, speak, react and change what they look like.

> SPRITE AREA

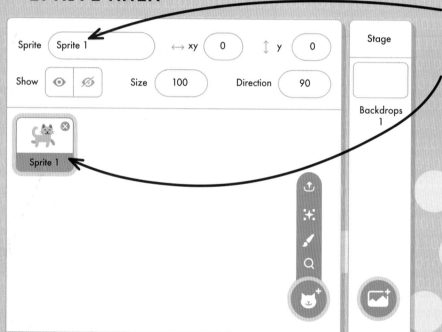

Each time you start a project the orange cat sprite will appear. This is automatically called Sprite 1, but you can **rename** it by highlighting the word 'Sprite 1' and typing a **more interesting name.**

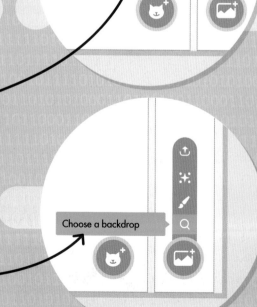

You can add sprites by hovering your mouse over the blue and white **'Choose a sprite'** button and then clicking the magnifying glass. There are **hundreds to choose** from. Click on a sprite and it will appear in your sprite list next to the cat. Sprites can be deleted by selecting them and then clicking the small 'x' in the blue circle.

Select a **backdrop** by hovering over the button and clicking the magnifying tool. Click on the 'forest' backdrop and it will appear on the stage.

> CODING AREA

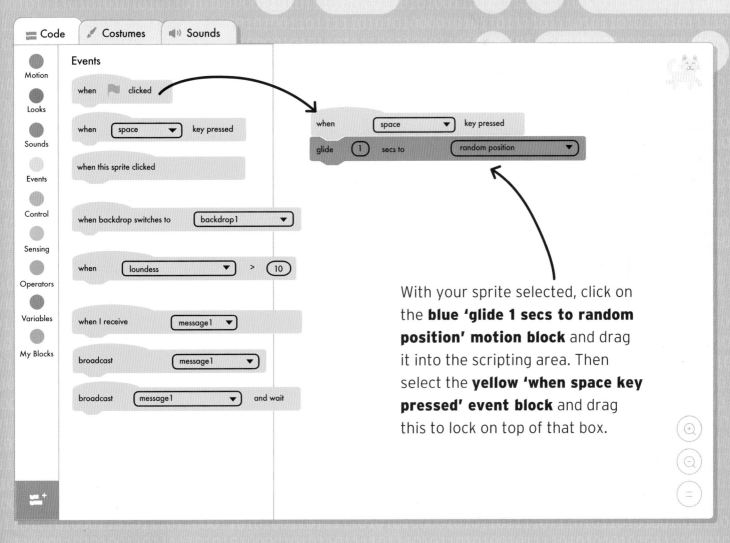

| Code | Costumes | Sounds |

Events

- when ⚑ clicked
- when space ▼ key pressed
- when this sprite clicked
- when backdrop switches to backdrop1 ▼
- when loudness ▼ > 10
- when I receive message1 ▼
- broadcast message1 ▼
- broadcast message1 ▼ and wait

Motion
Looks
Sounds
Events
Control
Sensing
Operators
Variables
My Blocks

when space ▼ key pressed
glide 1 secs to random position ▼

With your sprite selected, click on the **blue 'glide 1 secs to random position' motion block** and drag it into the scripting area. Then select the **yellow 'when space key pressed' event block** and drag this to lock on top of that box.

> STAGE AREA

Click the **green run flag** and press the space key on your keyboard. Your sprite will move randomly around the stage each time you press space! The stage can be enlarged by clicking the button with **four outward arrows** in the top right of the screen.

Play around with this simple project and get to know the Scratch interface a bit better.

The script you make can be changed (edited) by dragging the blocks away, or by sliding new blocks in. Individual blocks can be deleted by clicking on them and pressing delete, or just by dragging them back to the blocks palette. Try this...

Drag the **orange 'forever' control block** into your script. Drop it around the blue 'glide 1 secs to random position' motion block. Click where it says 'random position' and change it to 'mouse-pointer'.

Click the **green run flag**, press the space key and begin moving your mouse pointer around the stage. The cat will glide towards the mouse. The orange 'forever' control block means this will carry on every time the mouse moves.

You could also add the purple 'say hello for 2 seconds' looks block and the blue 'turn 15 degrees' motion block within the orange 'forever' control block.

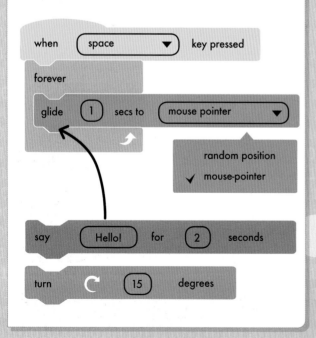

STARTING A PROJECT

Click 'File' and 'New' to start a new script, then give this easy project a name at the top.

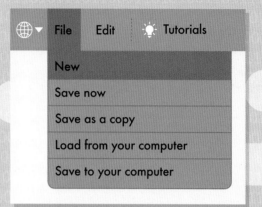

In your new project, place a **new sprite** in a **new backdrop**. Here the Shark 2 sprite is used with the Underwater 1 backdrop.

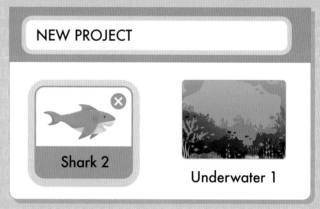

1 Click on the sprite, then move the yellow 'when space key is pressed' event block into the scripting area. Your aim is to **move the shark using your keyboard arrows.**

2 Change 'space' to 'up arrow' in your yellow event block. Place another yellow when space key pressed' event block in your scripting area and change 'space' to 'down arrow'.

3 **Drag the blue 'change y by 10' motion block** across to lock it into your first yellow event block. Add another blue 'change y by 10' motion block under it to the second yellow event block and in this one change '10' to '-10'. Using your **up and down keys** will now move the shark up and down!

4 To **move the shark right and left,** drag two more yellow 'when space key pressed' event blocks across. Change 'space' on one of them to 'right arrow' and stick a blue 'change x by 10' motionblock under it. Change the other to 'left arrow' and place a blue 'change x by 10' motion block to this too. Like before, change the value to '-10'.

5 The shark will now move right and left Remember to **click the green flag** to run your program.

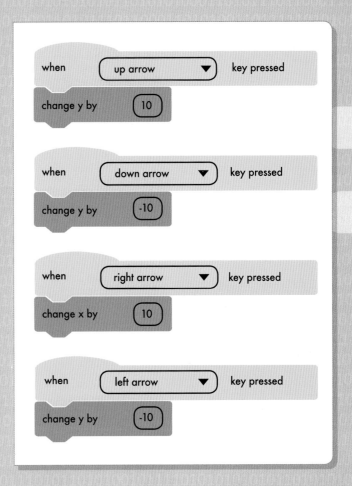

There doesn't need to be one script locked together in your script area to give instructions. These four bits of separate script **still make fully-working orders**.

Make it snappy, guys!

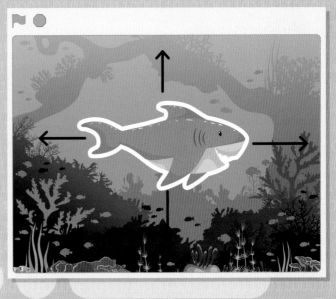

ANIMATING SPRITES

Now that you've created a shark that moves using the arrow keys, add an object (sprite) to this project for the shark to chase. Sounds scary, but it's simple!

1 Go to the 'Choose a sprite' button and **select the fish.**

Fish

2 With it highlighted in the sprite list, drag the blue 'glide 1 secs to random position' motion block across. Place the orange 'forever' control block around it and the yellow 'when green flag clicked' event block on top. The fish will **move randomly** around.

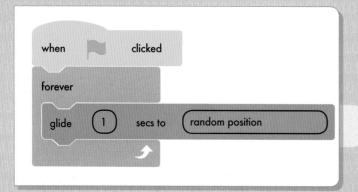

3 Click on your existing Shark 2 sprite. You can **alter the look or the pose** of a sprite. Drag the purple 'switch costume to shark2-a' looks block into the scripting area.

4 Place the orange 'wait 1 seconds' control block under it, followed by a purple 'switch costume' looks block set to 'shark2-b'. Put another orange 'wait 1 seconds' control block under that.

5 Place an orange 'forever' control block around it all and a yellow 'when green flag clicked' event block on the top. Run the script and the shark will **open and close** its mouth.

🖌 Costumes

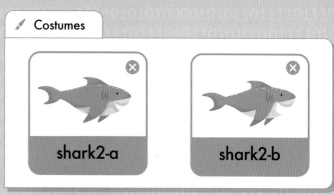

shark2-a   shark2-b

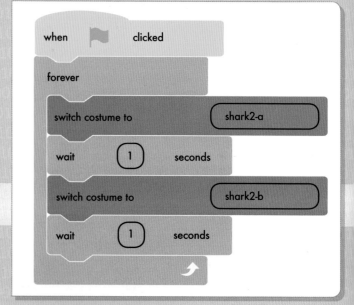

Move the shark with the arrow keys and it can now **chase the fish**... with chomping jaws!

CHANGE NUMBERS

In Scratch, the values and numbers connected with sprite blocks can be changed. For example, the gliding fish in the underwater scene could 'glide 5 secs to random position', which makes the fish slower. The 'y' and 'x' values that the shark moves when pressing the arrow keys can be changed to make it move more or less.

MOVE IT

The chomping shark can be scripted to chase the fish **without you having to move it**. With the shark 2 sprite selected, **delete the keyboard movement instructions** and place a script as shown here, but try changing 10 steps to 5 or 3.

BUBBLE TROUBLE

Now, if you want the shark to have a speech bubble, simply drag the **purple 'say Hello!' looks block** to under the purple 'switch costume to shark2-a' looks block. Another purple 'say Hello!' looks block could go under the second switch costume block. You can change the 'Hello!' text to 'Dinner!' if you like.

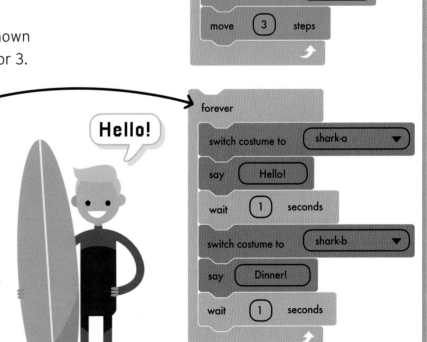

7 SUPER SPRITES TIPS

You've now got to grips with the basics of sprites, so these special tips will teach you even more!

> SIZING ISSUES

Sprites can be made bigger or smaller. Select a sprite, **change the number** in the size box and see that sprite change in the stage.

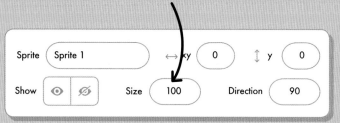

Sprite	Sprite 1	↔ x	0	↕ y	0

| Show | 👁 ⌀ | Size | 100 | Direction | 90 |

> DIY SPRITES

You can upload your own sprite image. Hover over the blue 'Choose a sprite' button, then **select the top arrow to upload something** from your desktop.

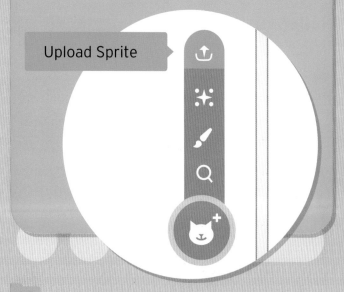

Upload Sprite

> NOW YOU SEE IT!

Click on a sprite and build the script below. It will **hide then reappear** on your backdrop. Change the number of seconds on the wait block to 5.

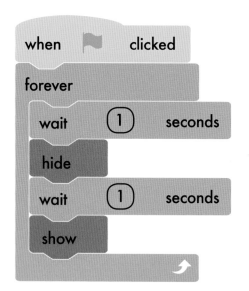

when ⚑ clicked

forever

wait (1) seconds

hide

wait (1) seconds

show

> FAVES

If you **love a sprite** you've selected and the script with it, you can easily copy it. Press the right click button on the sprite until 'duplicate, export, delete' appears. Then select 'duplicate'.

> YOU SPIN ME RIGHT ROUND!

Sprites can be made to move clockwise and anticlockwise. Put a 'turn 15 degrees' block inside a 'forever' block, with a 'green flag' block on top. Change the number to make it spin faster or slower.

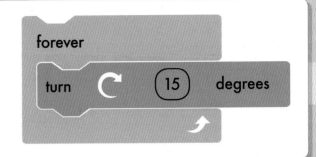

> ARTY FACTS

A sprite's appearance can be edited. Click the 'Costumes' tab in the top left and you'll see things like a paintbrush icon and a 'T' to add text to a sprite. For example you can **edit the cat** sprite to make its body and eyes bigger.

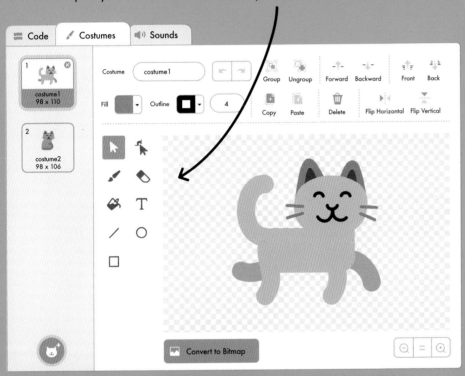

WOOF! WOOF!

> IN AN ORDERLY FASHION

Scripts always work in order from **top to bottom**. The top block will be the first instruction, with the bottom block last.

1st
2nd
3rd

THAT SOUNDS GOOD!

Sounds can make a chase game more fun, add an effect to an animation, or simply let a sprite create a silly noise!

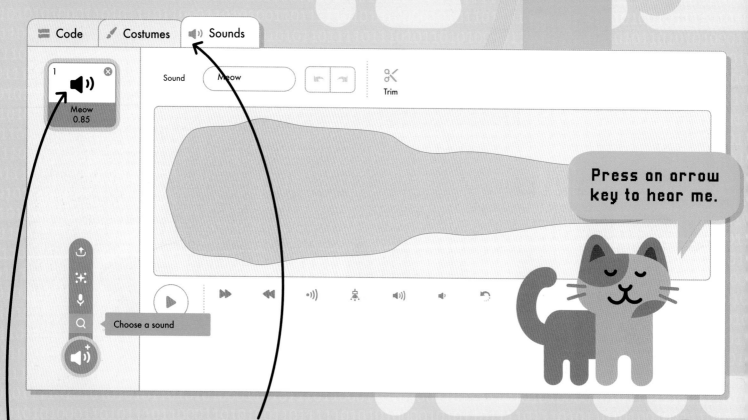

Press on arrow key to hear me.

Select a sprite, then click the 'Sounds' tab and hover your mouse over the blue speaker icon in the bottom left of the interface. Hit 'Choose a sound' to open the library and hover your mouse over them to listen.

Click on a sound and it will appear on the left of your sounds screen. **Effects like echo or robot can be added**, but ignore that for now. Select four sounds, then click the 'Code' tab and start a new project.

LISTEN AND LEARN

Each sprite has a sound. Put some sprites in your sprite list, click the sounds tab and play with the music or note a sprite makes.

START SOUND

Select a sprite and backdrop. Build this script, just as you did for the shark on page 16. This time, place 'start sound Meow' blocks under each, then select one of the **four new sounds** you chose in the library.

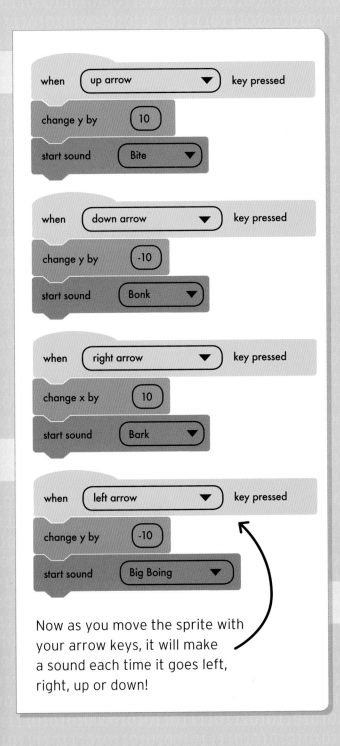

Now as you move the sprite with your arrow keys, it will make a sound each time it goes left, right, up or down!

SOUNDS AND MOVES

With your computer microphone, a Scratch script can be built so an **action will be taken** when a sound is detected.

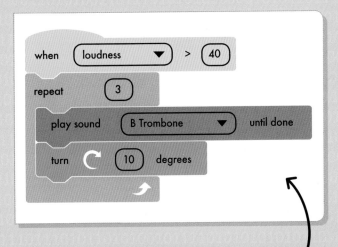

In a new project, place the **Cassy dance sprite** on the spotlight backdrop. Build this script that starts with a yellow 'when loudness > 10' event block and change 10 to 40. Add a sound to the purple 'play sound until done' sounds block (B Trombone is used here) so when Scratch detects a sound, the sprite makes noise and spins.

A-MAZE-ING!

It's time to build on your Scratch coding knowledge and create another fun script. Here you'll learn how to master a maze game.

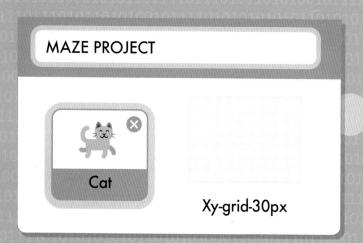

MAZE PROJECT

Cat

Xy-grid-30px

Choose a backdrop

1 Begin a new project by clicking 'File', then 'New' at the top left of the interface. Where it says 'Untitled', replace this with a new project name, such as 'MAZE PROJECT'.

2 Select the 'Xy-grid-30px' backdrop from the library. Put the cat in the top left of the stage, reducing its size to between 15 and 30, so it can fit in the maze!

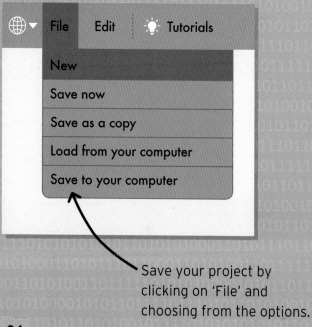

File   Edit   Tutorials

New
Save now
Save as a copy
Load from your computer
Save to your computer

Save your project by clicking on 'File' and choosing from the options.

Code   Backdrops   Sounds

3 Click on the backdrops stage (bottom right), then select the 'Backdrops' tab (top left) to begin drawing a maze. Make the maze lines **all one colour**. The lines here were made black by changing the 'Color', 'Saturation' and 'Brightness' levels in the fill tab.

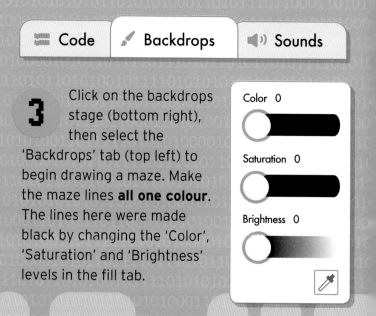

Color 0

Saturation 0

Brightness 0

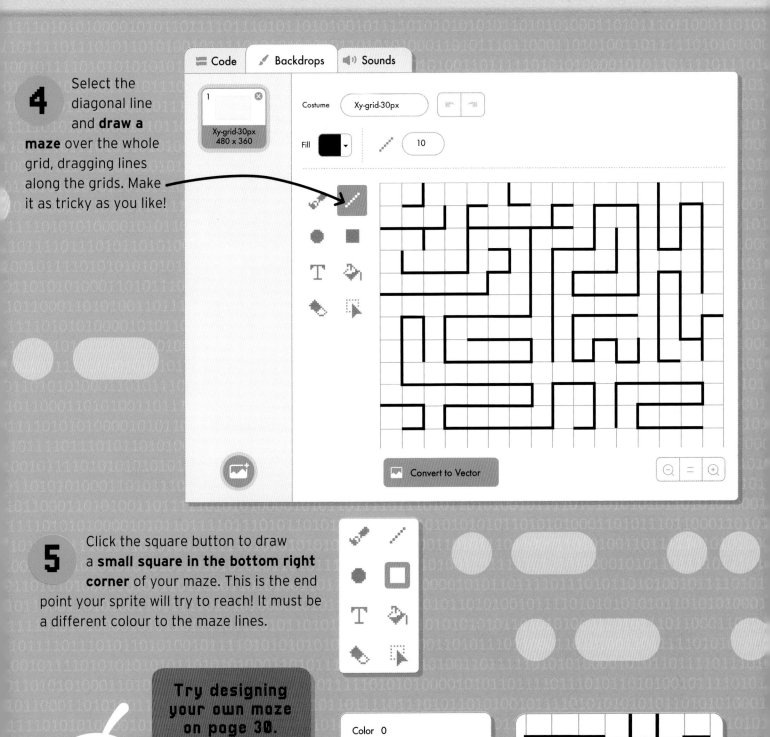

4 Select the diagonal line and **draw a maze** over the whole grid, dragging lines along the grids. Make it as tricky as you like!

5 Click the square button to draw a **small square in the bottom right corner** of your maze. This is the end point your sprite will try to reach! It must be a different colour to the maze lines.

Try designing your own maze on page 30.

Color 0

Saturation 100

Brightness 100

6 Time to script! With your cat sprite highlighted blue, build this code in the script area. This means you can **move the cat with your keys** (you will have to change the positive and negative values).

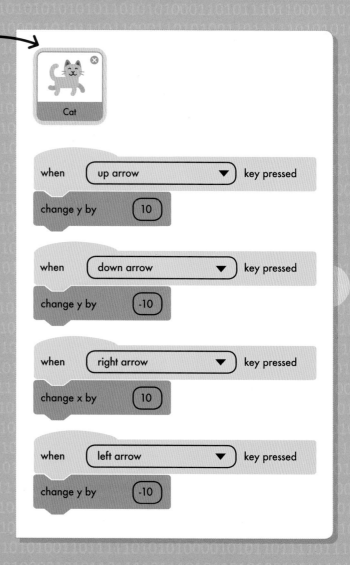

when [up arrow ▼] key pressed
change y by (10)

when [down arrow ▼] key pressed
change y by (-10)

when [right arrow ▼] key pressed
change x by (10)

when [left arrow ▼] key pressed
change y by (-10)

Cat

7 The script below will stop the cat being able to move over the black maze lines. The cat will always start in the top left corner, and if it touches a black line, it goes back to that spot!

A turquoise sensing block will stop the sprite being able to move over the black maze lines Place it inside an orange 'if' control block.

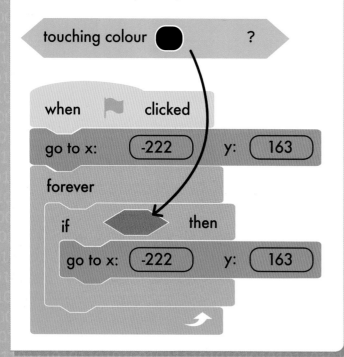

touching colour ● ?

when ⚑ clicked

go to x: (-222) y: (163)

forever

if ◇ then

go to x: (-222) y: (163)

To change the colour to the black of your maze lines, click the colour swatch and then the pipette displayed at the bottom. **Drag the enlarged circle** you now have over the maze in your stage, and click the small dot on one of the black lines. The colour shown in this sensing block will now change to black.

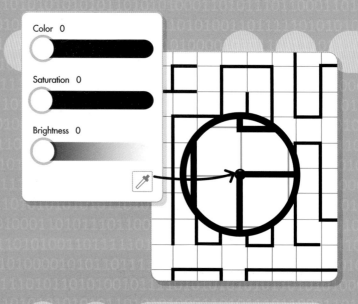

Color 0

Saturation 0

Brightness 0

8 You can now move the cat around the maze using the arrow keys. Next, add this to your sprite script... The red colour shown is the exact colour of the box at the finish. Add this to the turquoise 'touching colour' sensing block using the pipette, as before. The purple 'say You win! for 2 seconds' looks block was originally a purple 'say Hello! for 2 seconds' looks block. **Change 'Hello!' to any message you like!**

Practise moving the cat through the maze using arrow keys. Edit the backdrop maze to make it harder!

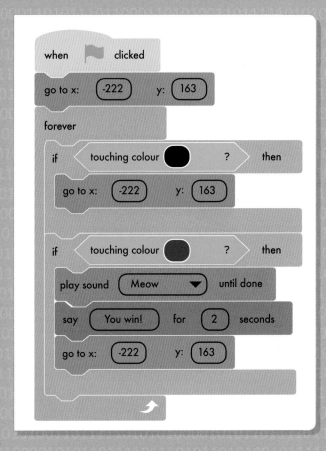

Your maze starts here.

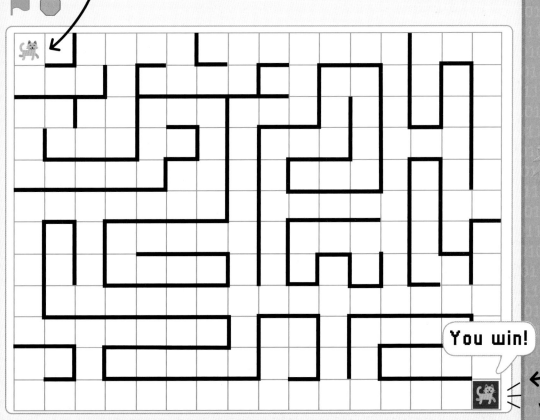

This square is where your cat wants to be!

You win!

Meow!

9 You can add another level to your maze so that when the end square is reached, a new backdrop appears and the maze continues! Build a new backdrop maze, like before. If you prefer, **try circles this time** instead of blocks and lines. Be sure to keep the circles or lines the same colour as your first maze so that the sensing blocks work.

10 Place 'switch backdrop to Xy-grid-30px' block under the green flag control block. Change the 'say You win! for 2 seconds' block in your script to 'say New level'. Add a purple 'next backdrop' looks block. The new maze will appear on screen. Remember to add a different coloured end square and win message at the end of your second maze.

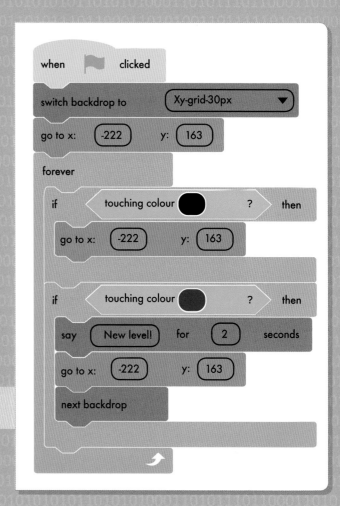

HAVE ANOTHER GO!
- - - - - - - - - - - - - - - -

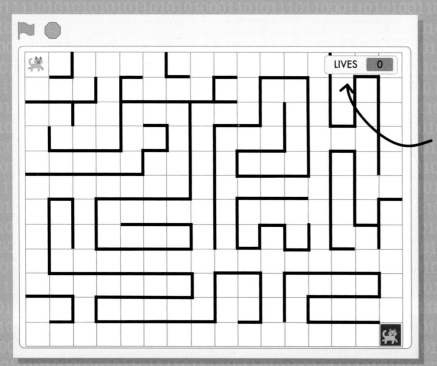

Dark orange 'Variables' blocks let Scratch users keep or store a value. The programmer sets this value. With your maze game, **variables can be used to make lives in the game.** If you run out of lives, the game is over!

Your lives are shown in this box. It appears on the stage area and can be moved around the maze.

Click on the **dark orange variables circle** in the list on the left of the interface. Then click in the box marked 'Make a Variable' and call it 'LIVES'. Keep the 'For all sprites' option checked.

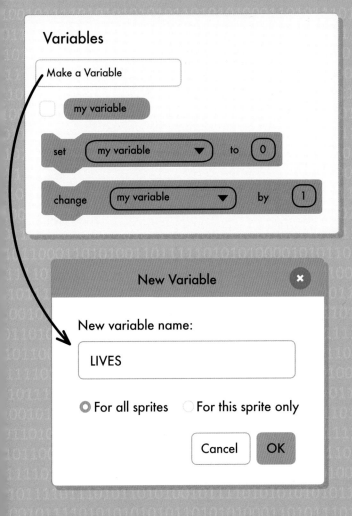

'LIVES' is now stored in a dark orange oblong above the other variables blocks.

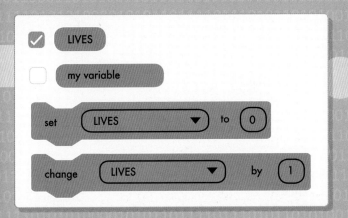

Add a dark orange 'set LIVES to 3' variables block under the yellow 'when green flag clicked' event block at the top. Place the dark orange 'change LIVES by -1' variables block as shown. Add an orange 'if' control block as shown below. Place a green '[blank] <1' operators block inside, then add a dark orange 'LIVES' oblong into the blank space.

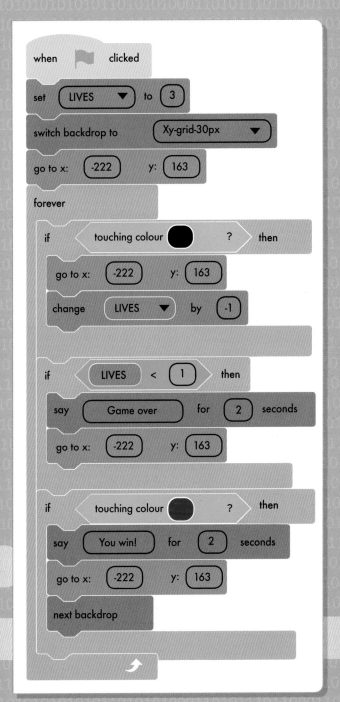

MAZE MAKER

Grab a pencil and use this space to plan out your own mazes.

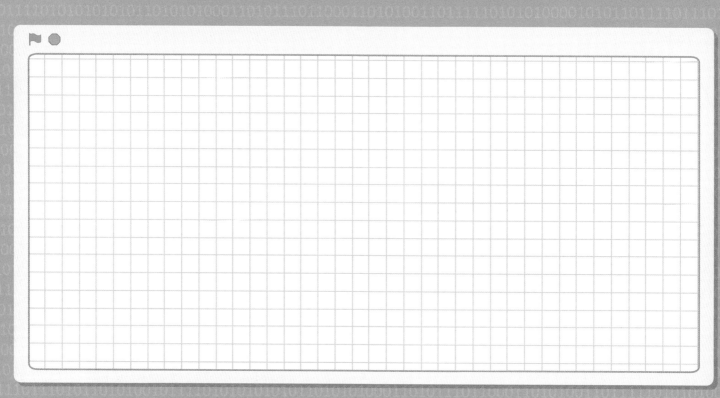

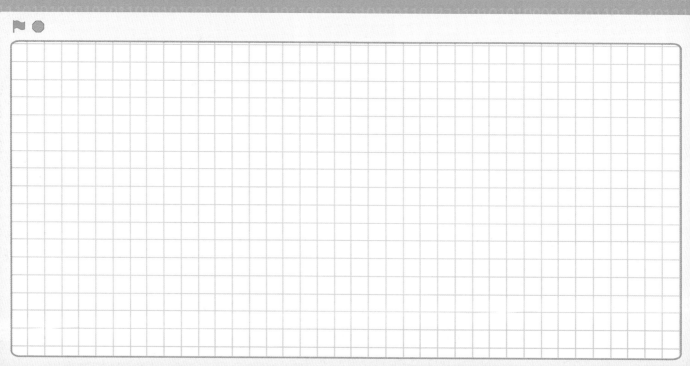

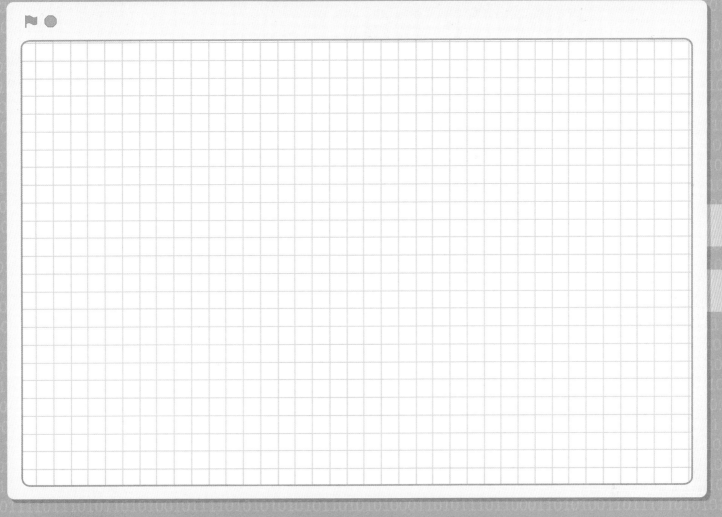

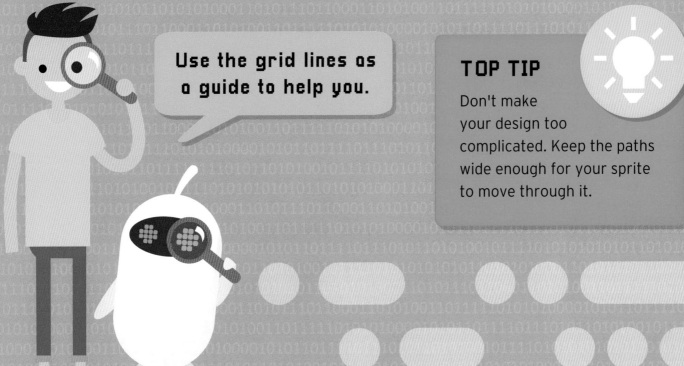

Use the grid lines as a guide to help you.

TOP TIP

Don't make your design too complicated. Keep the paths wide enough for your sprite to move through it.

SPACE RACE

This script lets you play a fun chase game and also includes your score, a timer, text and sound. You can pick your own sprites and backdrop, but our suggestions will get you started. Get ready – it's out of this world!

Space Race

Dot

Star

Xy-grid-30px

1 Begin a new project with a new project name, such as 'Space Race'.

2 Delete the cat sprite from your sprite list by clicking on the cross in the top right of its icon. Go to 'Choose a sprite' and select the **magnifying glass** tool. From the sprite library, select Dot the space dog.

3 Then select another sprite, called Star. Both sprites will now be in your sprite list. Also, select the galaxy backdrop from the backdrop library.

4 Highlight Dot so that there's a blue glow around the sprite. You need to make Dot smaller, so reduce the size from 100 to 50.

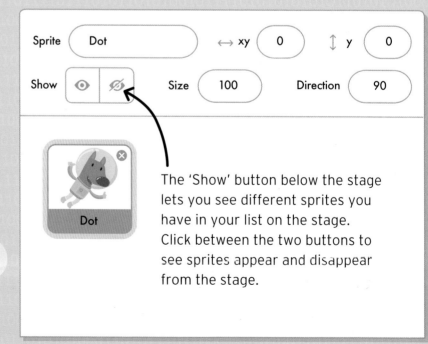

The 'Show' button below the stage lets you see different sprites you have in your list on the stage. Click between the two buttons to see sprites appear and disappear from the stage.

5 Create this simple script for Dot. Start with the purple 'say Hello! for 2 seconds' looks block, but change 'Hello!' to 'Time to chase stars!'. The blue 'glide 1 secs to mouse-pointer' motion block was originally 'glide 1 secs to random position'.

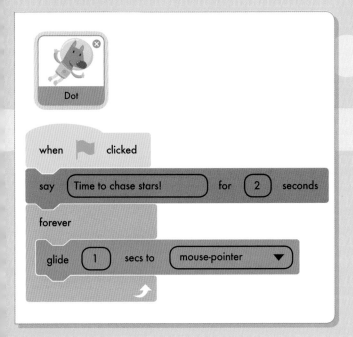

6 You need to **make a new variable for Dot**. Go to Variables, then click on the 'Make a Variable' box, type 'My score'. Click 'For all sprites', then 'OK'.

7 Write this second script for Dot. Select 'touching Star' from the turquoise sensing blocks (originally 'touching mouse-pointer'). When the game is ready, these instructions mean that each time Dot touches the star, he **gets a point and barks.** Cool!

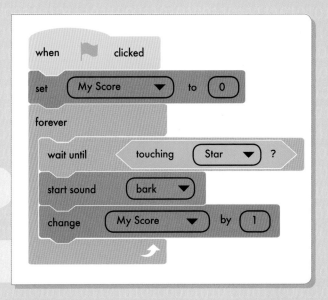

8 Highlight the star sprite. Move blocks across to the script area to build this code. It means that whenever Dot touches the star, the star moves to a new random position.

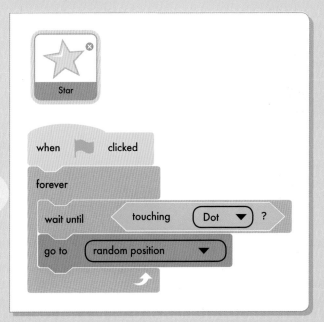

9 Next you must create a second new variable, like in step 6. Call it 'Timer'.

10 The star needs this second script. It sets up the countdown timer to appear under 'My Score' in the stage. The green 'Timer = 0' block comes from the Operators section. Place the dark orange 'timer' variables oblong inside it.

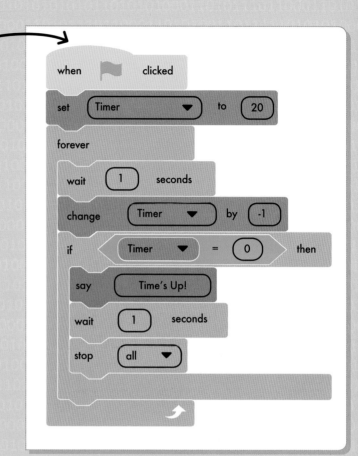

11 Set the timer tolal to 10, 20, 30, or however long you want to play. Click the green flag to run the script, place your mouse-pointer over the star and **see what score you get.** Let a friend have a go to see who does best!

LOOPS

In Scratch, the control blocks 'forever' and 'repeat' are known as **loops**. Loops are an instruction to keep doing part of a program.

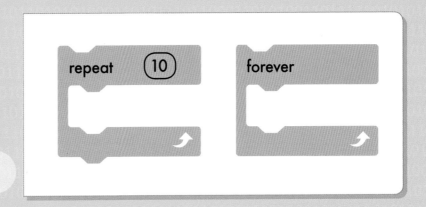

repeat (10)   forever

TOP TIP

If you create a script for one sprite and want another sprite in your list to have the same one, just **drag and drop** the script onto that sprite. Click on the second sprite and you'll see it has that code too.

Dot   Star

We are all running the 'play videogames' script!

MY STUFF

Scratch is a fantastic place to explore other users' programs, share scripts, ideas, knowledge and ask questions about your coding.

INTERFACE

From the Scratch interface, click your username in the top right and select 'My Stuff'. This takes you to **all the projects you've built**. If you've been following the suggestions in this book, 'Space Race' and the shark chasing game will be here.

Click 'See inside' by any of your projects and it appears on your screen. You can run the program again, or **make changes** if you've learnt new things since creating it.

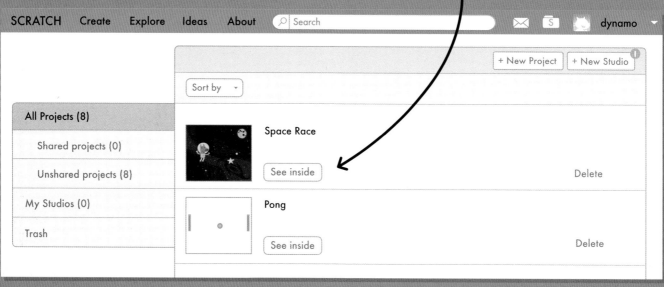

SCRATCH   Create   Explore   Ideas   About   🔍 Search   ✉   S   🐱 dynamo   ▾

+ New Project   + New Studio

Sort by ▾

All Projects (8)

Shared projects (0)

Unshared projects (8)

My Studios (0)

Trash

Space Race

See inside   Delete

Pong

See inside   Delete

PROFILE PAGE

- - - - - - - - - -

This section allows you to **write a bit about yourself.** Here you can say what Scratch projects you're building, and **'follow'** other Scratchers you like.

PROJECT PAGE

Click the project title on the 'My Stuff' list to get to the project page. Here you can share a project with the Scratch community so **others can play it and remix it.** Just click the orange 'Share' button in the top right.

Text boxes appear where you can write instructions to help people understand and enjoy your project. You can leave a **comment box** at the bottom for other users to share what they think. Click 'turn off commenting' if you don't want this function. When you know your way around 'My Stuff', the 'Studio' section lets you put lots of projects together.

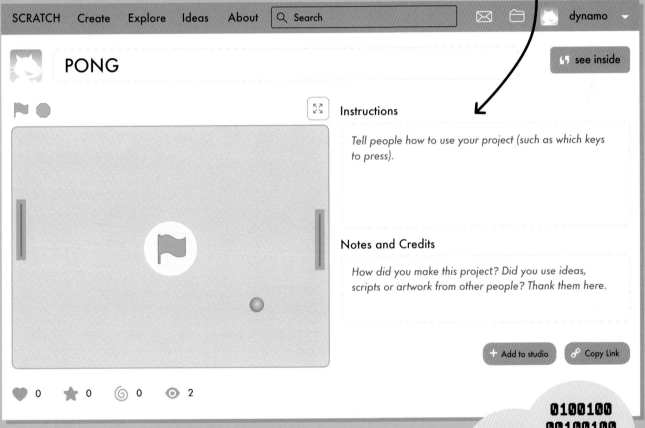

SCRATCH   Create   Explore   Ideas   About   Search   dynamo

PONG

see inside

Instructions

Tell people how to use your project (such as which keys to press).

Notes and Credits

How did you make this project? Did you use ideas, scripts or artwork from other people? Thank them here.

+ Add to studio   Copy Link

♥ 0   ★ 0   🌀 0   👁 2

DISCUSS STUFF

Go to the website **scratch.mit.edu/discuss** to view Scratch discussions and forums. You'll see announcements from the official Scratch team, plus projects, ideas, tips and stacks more!

PLAY PONG

Pong is a classic arcade game. A ball moves side-to-side and players move a paddle up and down to keep the ball in play. If the ball moves beyond your paddle, the other player scores a point. Here you'll learn how to build a clever script to play pong.

1 Create a new project and name it Pong. Delete the scratch cat sprite and add the ball from the sprite library.

Pong

Ball   Paddle

2 Make this script for the ball. Click the green flag to run it and see the ball move from side-to-side.

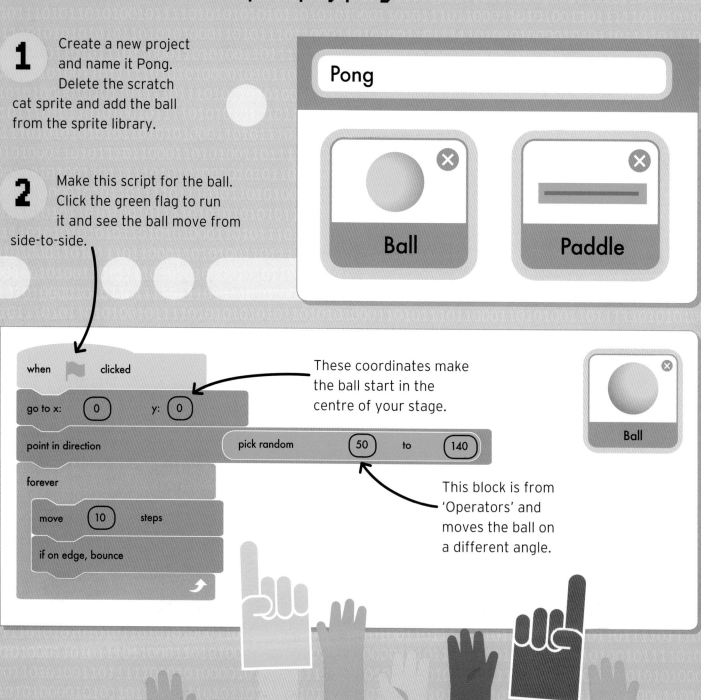

when ⚑ clicked

go to x: 0   y: 0

point in direction   pick random 50 to 140

forever

move 10 steps

if on edge, bounce

These coordinates make the ball start in the centre of your stage.

This block is from 'Operators' and moves the ball on a different angle.

Ball

3 Place the green paddle sprite in your sprite list. With the paddle highlighted blue, click on the 'Costumes' tab, and then the small arrow in the top left. Click your mouse over the small, double-headed blue arrow. Slowly **rotate the paddle** so it's upright and not horizontal.

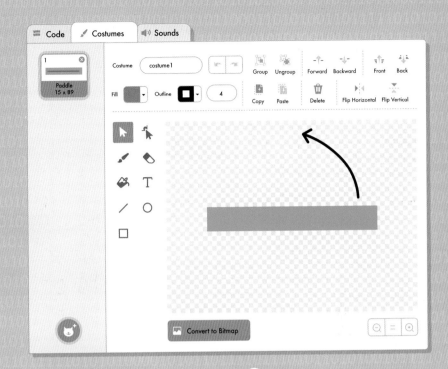

4 With the paddle still selected, click the 'Code' tab to begin its script. Drag these blocks across to start your script.

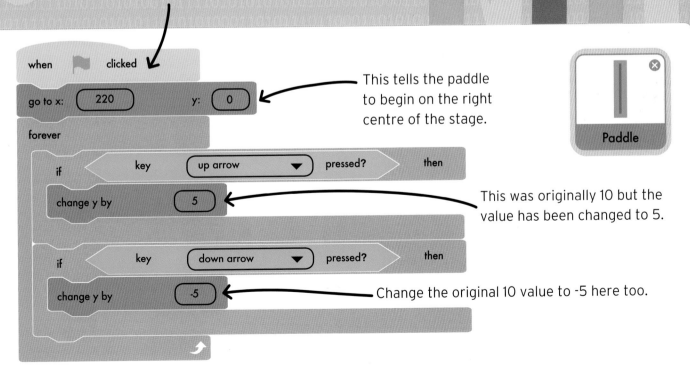

This tells the paddle to begin on the right centre of the stage.

This was originally 10 but the value has been changed to 5.

Change the original 10 value to -5 here too.

Paddle

5 The extra bits of code below **stop the paddle moving off** the stage. To place your turquoise 'key up arrow pressed' sensing block in the green 'and' operators block, put the 'and' operators block under your script. Drag the turquoise 'key up arrow pressed' sensing block away from your script, and **into the first space** on the green 'and' operators block.

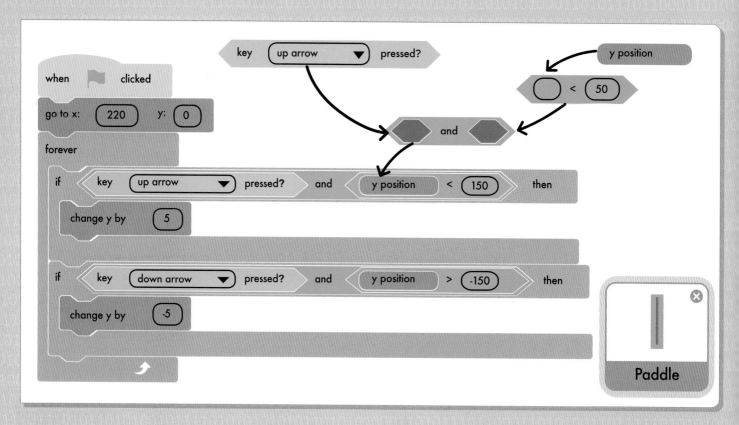

6 Now you need a green '< 50' operators block. Place this inside the second dark green space and change '50' to '150'. Do the same for the 'down arrow key' block, using the 'y position' block and changing the value to '-150'. **Remember to make this a negative value.**

7 Pong needs two paddles, one on each side of the stage. Right click on the paddle button in your sprites list and 'duplicate, export, delete' options will appear. Select 'duplicate' and the **exact same paddle will appear**. It will automatically be called 'Paddle2'.

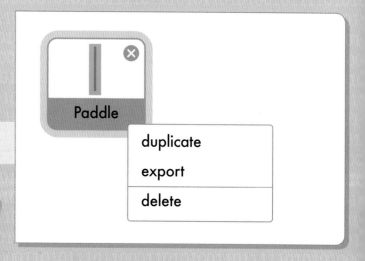

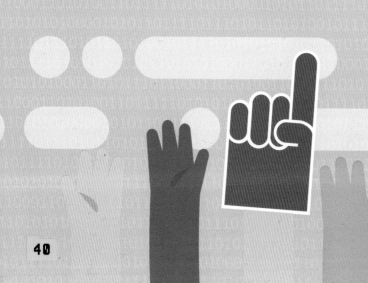

8 Change paddle2's 'go to x220 y0' block at the top of its script to '-220'. Paddle2 will be controlled by a second player. For paddle2, change where it says 'up' and 'down' to 'w' and 'x'. Player 2 will move Paddle2 up and down by these keys.

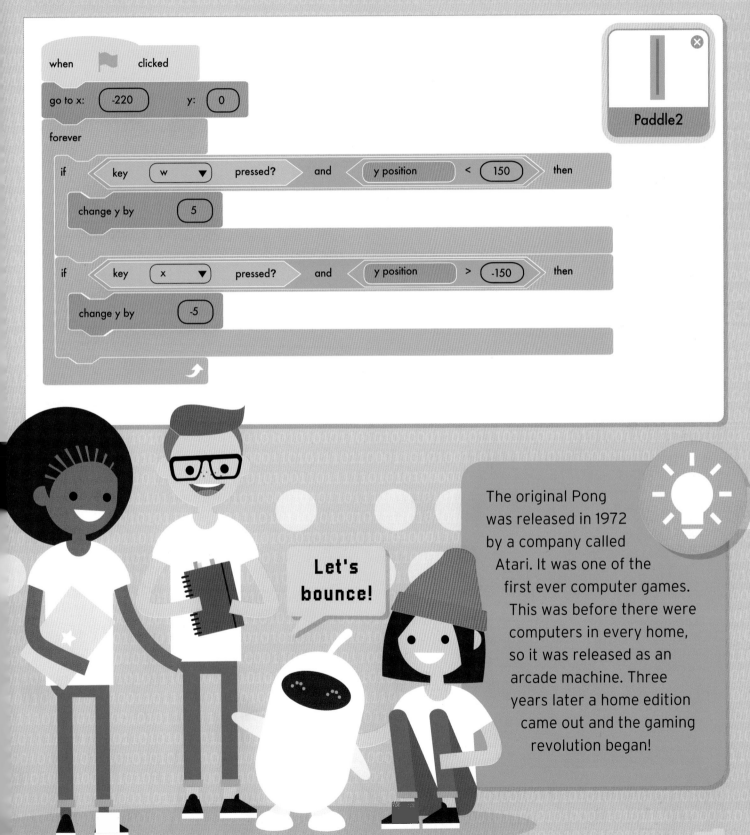

Let's bounce!

The original Pong was released in 1972 by a company called Atari. It was one of the first ever computer games. This was before there were computers in every home, so it was released as an arcade machine. Three years later a home edition came out and the gaming revolution began!

9 Make the paddle 'hit' the ball and send it back in a different direction. Select the ball script from step 1 and place 'if', 'touching' and 'point in direction' blocks to it. For the touching block, switch 'mouse-pointer' to 'Paddle'. To make the 'point in direction' block as shown, place a green multiplier operators block where it says '90'. Now stick a 'direction' block inside this and make the value '-1'.

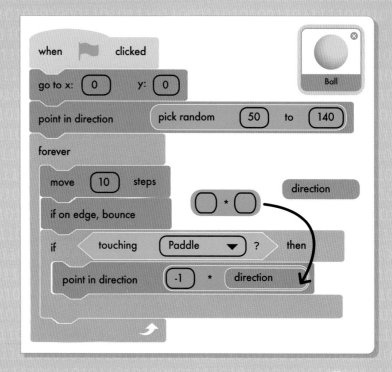

10 Change the ball's script so that Paddle2 also bounces the ball back. Select the ball's script, then drag out the 'touching Paddle ?' block from its script and place it on your script area. Put it inside a green 'or' operators block, then the 'touching Paddle ?' block in the first box, like this. Go to a 'touching mouse-pointer' sensing block and change it to 'Paddle2'. Drag this into the other side of your 'or' operators block. Place this whole block back into the ball's script, in the 'if' section, like this.

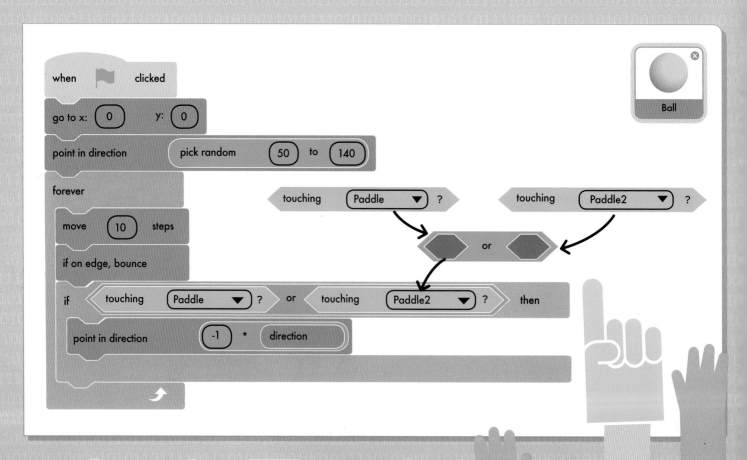

Time to **add scoring** to your pong game. The program needs to know that if the ball moves beyond the paddle on the right, Player 2 gets a point. If it moves beyond the left paddle, Player 1 wins a point.

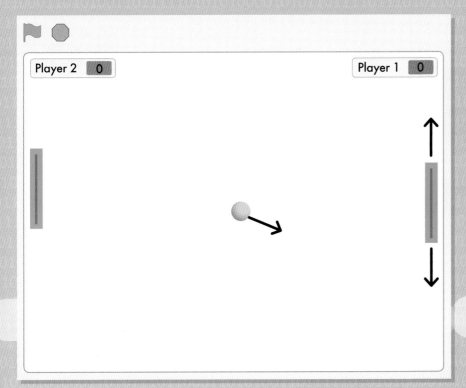

11 Highlight the ball script. In the stage, click on the ball and drag it to the right so that it almost touches the edge of the screen. Then click the box beside the 'x position' motion block. **The ball's x position value is now displayed** at the top of the stage.

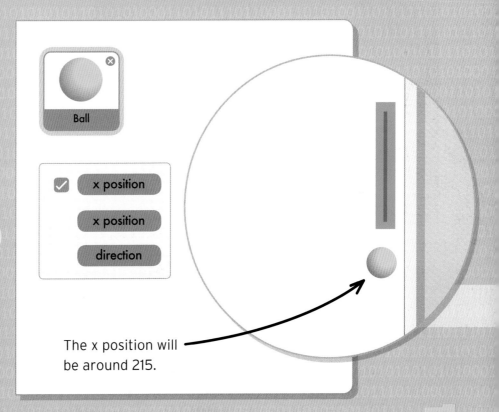

The x position will be around 215.

12 Add to the ball's script to include this program. This means that if the ball touches the right or left edge, a point is awarded.

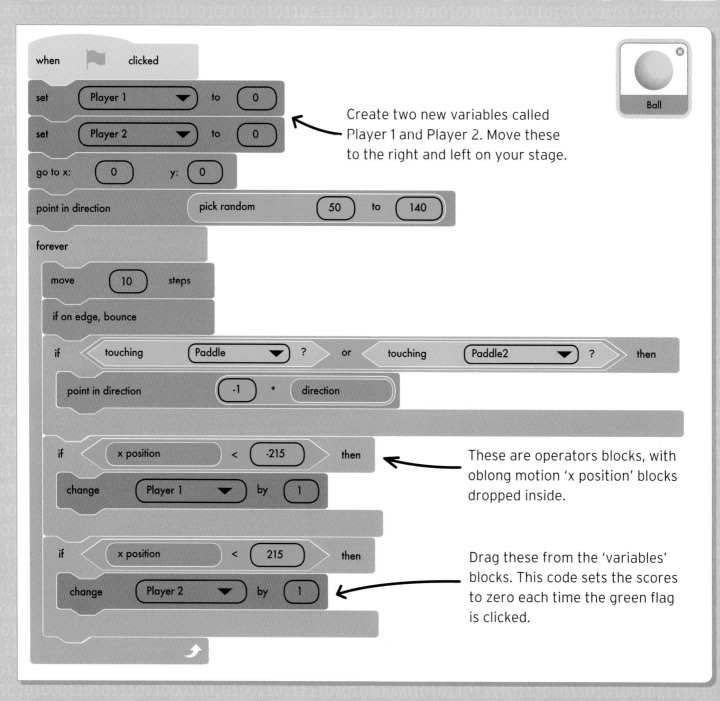

Create two new variables called Player 1 and Player 2. Move these to the right and left on your stage.

These are operators blocks, with oblong motion 'x position' blocks dropped inside.

Drag these from the 'variables' blocks. This code sets the scores to zero each time the green flag is clicked.

13 You can create an 'event' to place the ball in the centre of the stage when a point is scored. First split your ball's script into two chunks after the 'go to x0 y0' block.

14 Drag a yellow 'broadcast message1' event block to the bottom of the green flag section of script. Click the text, 'message1' and create a new message called 'Start!'

15 Add 'when I receive Start!' and 'go to x0 y0' to the top of the other part of the script, like this. Place two 'broadcast Start!' blocks in the bottom two 'if' parts, as shown here. Run the program and when a point is scored, the ball will move from the centre of the stage.

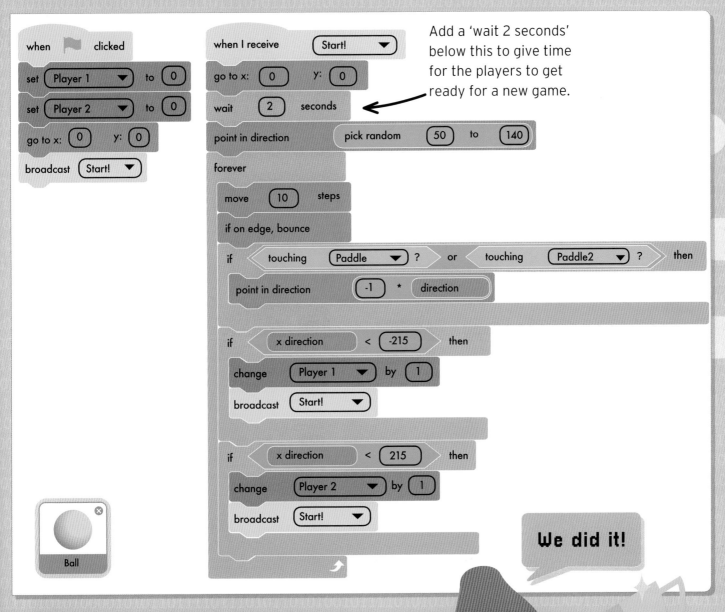

Add a 'wait 2 seconds' below this to give time for the players to get ready for a new game.

We did it!

Experiment and play around with your pong game. Add a backdrop, such as neon tunnel or wall 1, to make it extra cool. You can add a countdown timer (see page 32) to make it more exciting. Edit the speed that the ball moves, how much the paddles move and even the size of the paddles.

MAKING SENSE OF SCRATCH

Never turn on your webcam without checking with an adult first!

If your computer has a webcam, Scratch has some super-smart moves using video sensing to carry out epic actions. With a simple wave of your hands you can play music, make a cat meow or pop a balloon!

Click on the 'add extension' button in the bottom left of the interface. Several extension options appear, such as music, pen and translate. Click on 'Video Sensing' and this option appears on the left side of your screen.

Video Sensing

Your webcam will be turned on and some new blocks appear under the video sensing header.

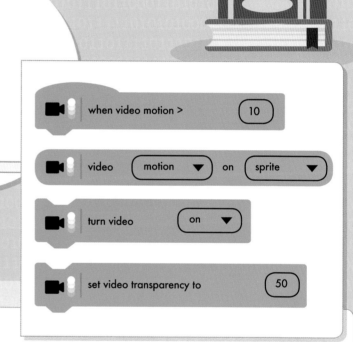

when video motion >   10

video   motion ▼   on   sprite ▼

turn video   on ▼

set video transparency to   50

Cat

WAVE

With your cat sprite selected, drag these two blocks into your script area. Wave your hand (or your head!) towards the cat in your webcam, where the stage usually is, and it will meow. Cute, eh?

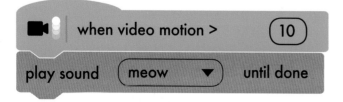

when video motion >   10

play sound   meow ▼   until done

Change the value '10' from the 'when video motion' block to 50 or 90. You'll spot that the sound sensitivity changes so you have to wave harder or nearer to the cat to make it meow.

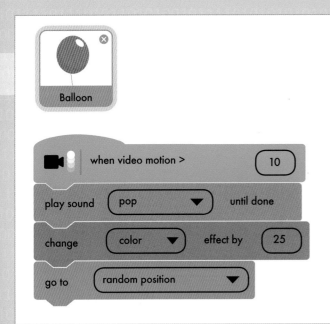

BALLOON FUN

Delete the cat sprite and select the balloon from the sprite library. With the balloon selected, build this script. Run it and each time you wave at, or pop, the balloon, it **makes a sound and appears in a different spot** in a new colour. Increase the video motion value from 10 to make the webcam less sensitive.

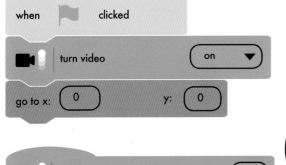

BASKETBALL

With video sensing you can move objects around your stage. In a new project, delete the cat sprite and **select the basketball.** Highlighting the basketball sprite, create this script. Change the coordinates on the 'go to x y' block to 0 and 0.

To build the 'point in direction video direction on sprite' block, place this block over where it says '90' and drop it in.

Move your hands to the basketball and **push it around** the stage. Get someone else in front of the webcam with you to push the ball between you!

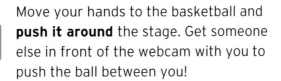

ROCK OUT

Scratch can make your dreams come true and turn you into a rock star. Start a new project and delete the cat sprite. In the sprite library, click the music option and **select two drums** to add to your sprite list. Here we've used Drum and Drum Kit.

Click on one of your sprites and build this script. Switch costume options for your drum, which are 'drum-b' and 'drum-a' here. Do exactly the same for your other drum, remembering to **switch costumes** for that too.

Place the drums in the corners of the stage. When you **wave your hands over them, they will make a drum sound** and move as though they've been hit. Rock on, dudes!

Drum

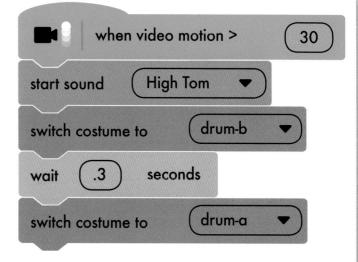

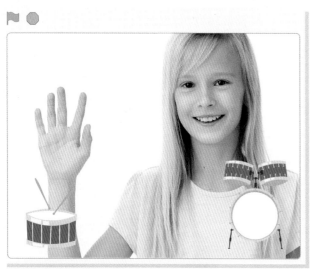

Drum Kit

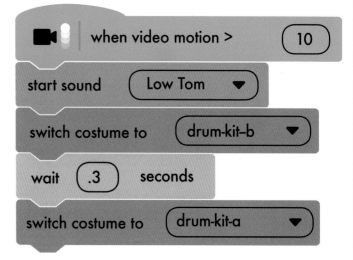

WAVE IT AWAY

Here's a neat way to wave goodbye to scary sights! Using purple 'looks' blocks to change effects, **video sensing can make sprites gradually disappear** from your screen. Build this code to make ghosts and ghouls vanish...

1 Start a new project named 'Spooky Wave' and select the ghost sprite. This code will work with any sprite you choose but the ghost is a fun one to begin with.

2 With your sprite highlighted, drag these two blocks across. At first the 'colour' option will be selected in this 'looks' block. Change it to 'ghost' by clicking on it and selecting from the dropdown options.

3 In 'Variables' name a new variable from 'Make a variable' called 'Wipe'. This then appears as a new option in an orange oblong shape, below the 'My variable' oblong.

4 From the video sensing blocks, **begin a new piece of code for the sprite** with the 'when video motion > 10' block and continue like this. The 'change ghost effect by 10' will originally be 'change color effect by 25' in the 'looks' selection on the left.

5 To build the 'if Wipe > 95 then' block, drag these three blocks into your script area. Drop 'Wipe' onto the green operators block and change the value to 50. This can be placed in the 'if then' block.

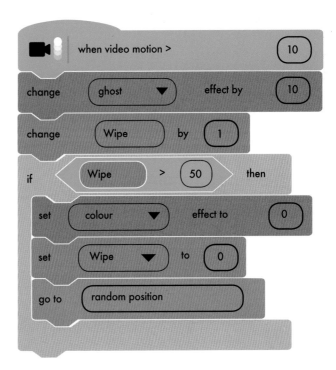

6 Click the green flag run button. Rub your hand over the ghost and it will gradually fade away from your screen. Awesome!

STORY TIME

Scratch lets you build your own story. You can tell a story about anything you like – about space, sport, history or something in your own life, using the Scratch sprites and backdrops. A mix of text, sound and animation will bring your imagination to life!

Use this space to map out your story!

Circle a setting from below, or write your own:

Castle   Forest   The Moon   Jungle   School

Character 1's name:

Character 2's name:

Setting 2:

Castle   Forest   The Moon   Jungle   School

Animal:

Owl   Tiger   Beetle

Write down some ideas for the plot...

STORY

Wizard   Dani   Owl   Forest   Woods

1 Start a new Scratch project and name it 'Story'. Delete the cat sprite and select a new backdrop from the backdrop library. Here the 'Forest' backdrop is selected.

2 Select any two sprites, such as the wizard and Dani. The sprites may not be facing each other. Click on the sprite you want to change direction, then their 'Costume' tab and the 'Flip Horizontal' button to turn them the opposite way.

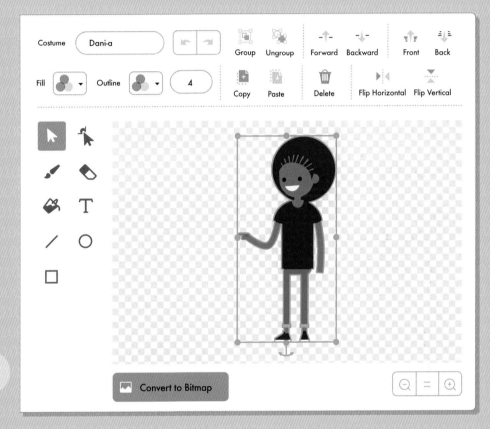

3 Click the sprite you want to begin your story with. Make sure the 'Code' tab in the top left is selected for this sprite. For the wizard sprite, **type whatever you like over the top of 'Hello!'** in the 'say' looks block.

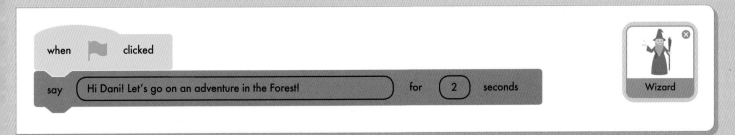

4 Click on the other sprite. Build the same script as in step 3, but type a sentence to respond to the wizard. Add a 'wait 1 second' block and change the value to '2 seconds'. Run the script and the **sprites will talk to each other** using your text bubbles.

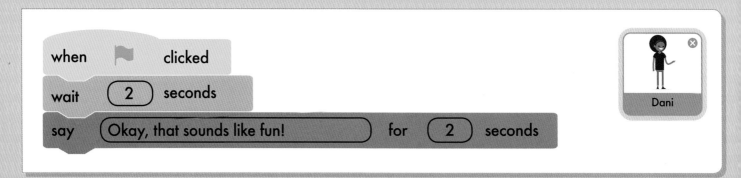

when ⚑ clicked
wait (2) seconds
say (Okay, that sounds like fun!) for (2) seconds

Dani

Hi Dani! Lets go on an adventure in the Forest!

Okay, that sounds like fun!

You can now make your sprites appear in a new location and carry on the story. Select another backdrop, such as 'Woods'.

5 With the wizard sprite highlighted, add this code into that sprite's script area. Select 'Forest' and 'Woods' from each of the 'switch backdrop to' block options. Run the code and the backdrop will change.

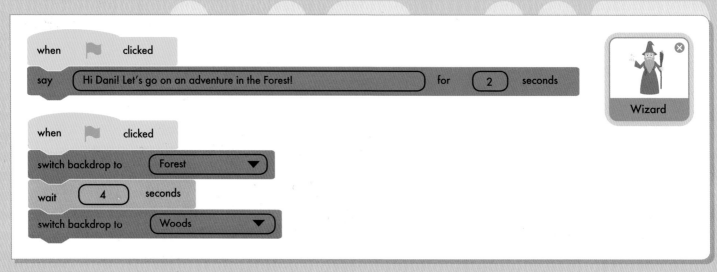

when ⚑ clicked
say (Hi Dani! Let's go on an adventure in the Forest!) for (2) seconds

when ⚑ clicked
switch backdrop to (Forest ▼)
wait (4) seconds
switch backdrop to (Woods ▼)

Wizard

6 Next, create a story break to sit between the first two scenes. Select the 'choose a backdrop' button, bottom right, and click on 'paint'.

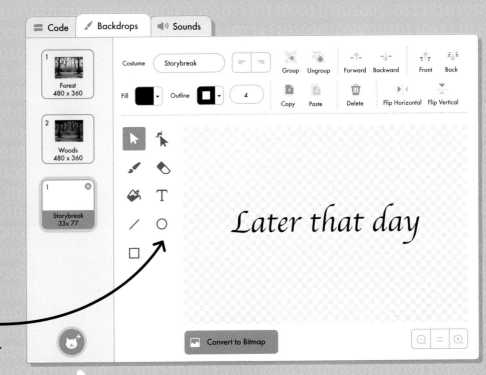

7 Click the 'T' tool and type 'Later that day' into the centre of the blank backdrop. The arrow tool makes the text box bigger. Name this backdrop 'storybreak'.

Here you can play around with fonts, plus the size and colour of your text.

Wolkies!

8 Click the wizard sprite, and with the 'Code' tab selected, extend the script, like this.

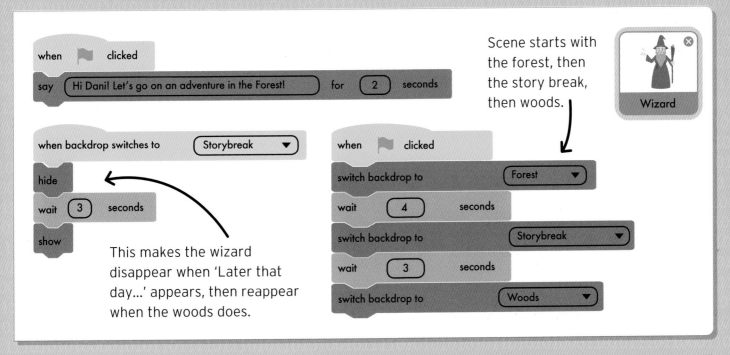

Scene starts with the forest, then the story break, then woods.

Wizard

when 🏳 clicked

say Hi Dani! Let's go on an adventure in the Forest! for 2 seconds

when backdrop switches to Storybreak ▼

hide

wait 3 seconds

show

This makes the wizard disappear when 'Later that day...' appears, then reappear when the woods does.

when 🏳 clicked

switch backdrop to Forest ▼

wait 4 seconds

switch backdrop to Storybreak ▼

wait 3 seconds

switch backdrop to Woods ▼

9 Do the same for Dani's script. This sprite must 'hide' and 'show' too. Run the script. With these simple rules and instructions, you can add new text bubbles and backdrops as you like.

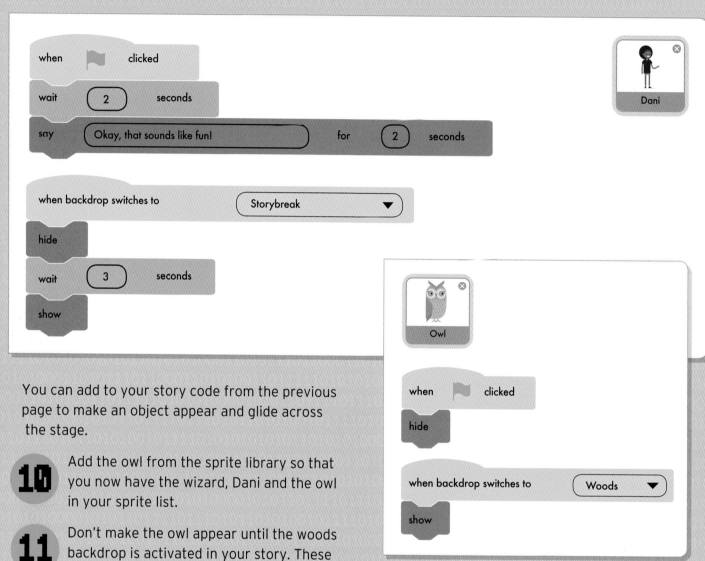

when 🏳 clicked

wait (2) seconds

say (Okay, that sounds like fun!) for (2) seconds

when backdrop switches to (Storybreak ▼)

hide

wait (3) seconds

show

Dani

Owl

when 🏳 clicked

hide

when backdrop switches to (Woods ▼)

show

You can add to your story code from the previous page to make an object appear and glide across the stage.

10 Add the owl from the sprite library so that you now have the wizard, Dani and the owl in your sprite list.

11 Don't make the owl appear until the woods backdrop is activated in your story. These two bits of code for the owl do just that!

12 Select the owl sprite. Click the owl in the stage and drag it to the top left of the stage. Next click the 'motion' tool and the x and y coordinates now show the owl's position.

13 Add this motion block to the script. **The owl appears** at the top when the backdrop changes to the woods.

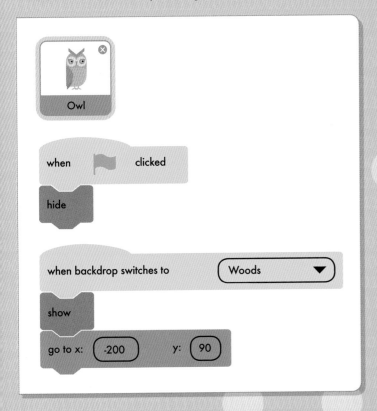

14 Click on the owl in the stage and drag it to Dani. The x and y coordinates for the owl will change in the motion blocks down the left of the interface.

15 Drag the 'glide 1 secs to x y' block (this will have different coordinates to the other motion block in this script) across and complete the code, like this. **Run it and the owl will appear, then fly down to Dani.**

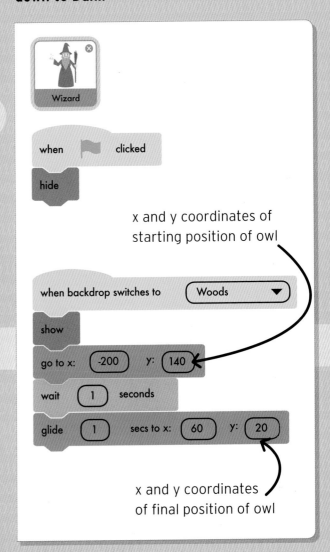

x and y coordinates of starting position of owl

x and y coordinates of final position of owl

To-doooo!

 # SCRATCH SKILLS

Now you know how Scratch works and what you can create in code. Here are a few more things to try out and explore!

RECORD SOUNDS

It's easy to drop a sound recording you've made into your script. Choose a sprite, then click the 'Sounds' tab for it at the top left of the interface.

Click the red 'Record' button and speak to make the sound you want. Click 'Save' and **name your new sound,** then press return on your keyboard.

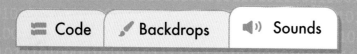

Select 'Record' from the bottom left of the interface.

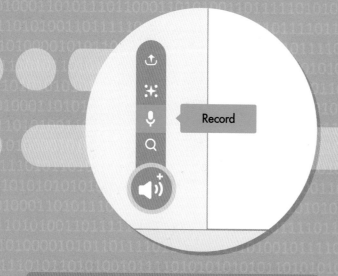

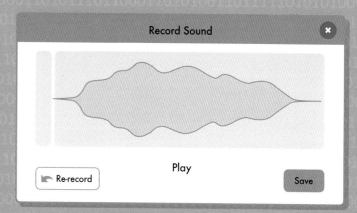

This new sound can be selected from the dropdown choices in the purple 'sound' blocks, and added to the script.

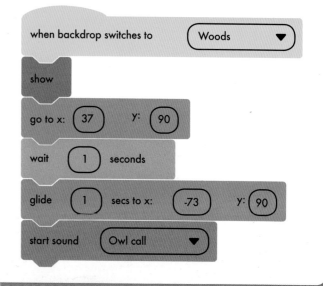

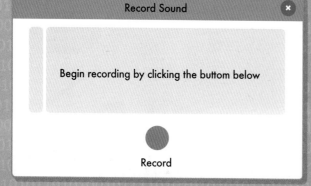

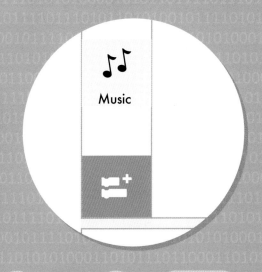

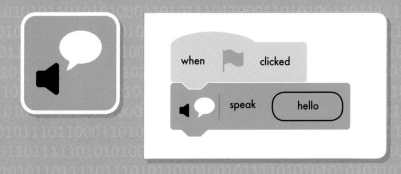

TEXT TO SPEECH

Make sprites talk using the 'Text to Speech' section, found through the Extensions button. Click on a new project and pick a sprite, then **add speech to the sprite** with these two simple blocks. Use your new skills from this book to make a speaking story.

MAKE MUSIC

Open the 'Music' option through the Extensions button to **make your own sounds** and tunes. This example script uses different drums played in a quick repeat pattern. Try out your own music-making ideas and add them to games!

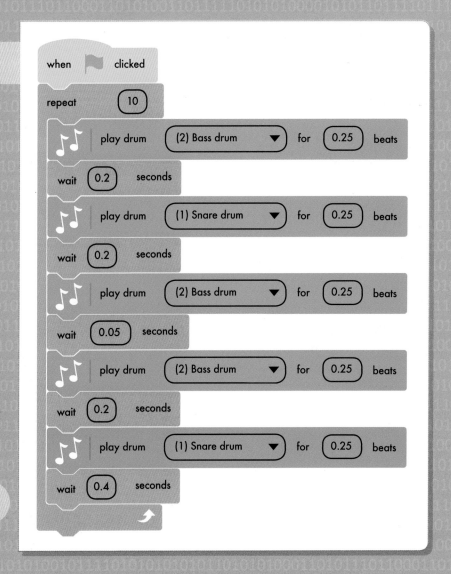

La la la la! Making music is the best!

>>> PYTHON

Another programming language, called Python, is trickier to understand, but is very effective and powerful once you get to know it. Huge companies and groups like Google, Netflix and the NHS in Britain use it.

Python uses text, such as letters, numbers, punctuation and symbols, and not blocks. Python code must be written correctly so that the computer understands it – capital letters, brackets and full stops must all be in the right place! It uses a program called IDLE, which stands for Integrated Development and Learning Environment. IDLE has a text editor that lets you write and change coding.

PYTHON: REASONS WHY IT ROCKS!

1 It's free! Just like Scratch, Python can be downloaded without charge. It was developed by Guido van Rossum, a Dutch programmer, in the early 1990s.

2 Python can be used easily on Windows PCs and Mac computers.

3 There are lots of Python coding libraries. Often you can quickly use this code, rather than making your own.

INSTALLING

Python needs to be downloaded and installed to your computer. Go to **www.python.org**, click on the Downloads tab at the top and then Windows or Mac, depending on what computer you have.

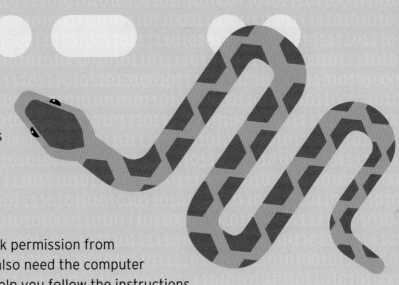

WWW.PYTHON.ORG

Carefully follow the instructions to download it. Ask permission from the computer owner before you do this. You may also need the computer owner to type in a password to allow this, and to help you follow the instructions.

As you work through the download process, you should be able to double click the Python installer file. It may look like this, depending on whether you use a PC or Mac...

...then the **IDLE** icon. If the download has been successful, the Python window should open. It looks something like this...

Python 3.7.2 Shell

```
Python 3.7.2 (v3 7.2:9a3ffc0492, Dec 24 2018, 02:44:43)
[Clang 6.0 (clang-600.0.57] on darwin
Type "help", "copyright", "credits" or "license()" for more information.
>>>
```

> PLAY WITH PYTHON

Now that you've installed it, open up IDLE on your computer. Python has two windows – the 'code window' and the 'shell window'. These two windows look very similar, but make sure you know which is which and keep them separate on your computer screen.

> SHELL WINDOW

Python 3.7.2 Shell

```
Python 3.7.2 (v3 7.2:9a3ffc0492, Dec 24 2018, 02:44:43)
[Clang 6.0 (clang-600.0.57] on darwin
Type "help", "copyright", "credits" or "license()" for more information.
>>>
```

When IDLE opens, the shell window appears first. For a beginner you'll find that most code must be typed into the code window, with the output (result of the coding) appearing in the shell. Python code typed in the shell window shows the output instantly.

In the shell window, click on 'File' at the top and then 'New File'.

| IDLE | File | Edit | Shell | Debug | Options | Window | Help |

New File
Open...
Open Module...
Recent Files
Module Browser
Path Browser

Close
Save
Save As...
Save Copy As...

> CODE WINDOW

The code window will appear. Type this code into it...

```
print ('Good morning, Python!')
```
Ln: 1   Col:29

Print is the same as the 'say' block in Scratch. Make sure it's all lower case.

Use single quote marks inside brackets and type your message between them.

When you've written this code, click on 'File', then 'Save As' and name the file 'GoodMorning'. Next go to the 'Run' tab and click 'Run Module'.

| IDLE | File | Edit | Format | Run | Options | Window | Help |

Python Shell
Check Module
Run Module

Your Python code will appear in your shell window. Well done - you've programmed and executed your first Python code!

```
Good morning, Python!
>>>
```

Python code will not 'run' successfully unless it has been saved in the code window. Make sure you save work regularly. An error message may display when you click 'Run Module'. Usually this means you have made a spelling or typing mistake in your code. Even the slightest error, like using a full stop instead of a colon, will mean it won't run. **Always type code carefully.**

| IDLE | File | Edit | Shell | Debug |

New File
Open...
Open Module...
Recent Files
Module Browser
Path Browser

Close
Save

Save As...
Save Copy As...

> WORD PLAY

Python is a coding language you'll need to learn and understand to type correctly and to form instructions. Here are some basic words and commands, and what they do, to give you an idea of how Python looks and works.

1
```
print ('Hello everyone!')
```
= the words within the brackets and single quotes appear in your program.

2
```
while True:
    print ('Hello!')
```
Make an indent here.

= say hello forever, like the 'forever' loop in Scratch.

3
```
for i in range (10):
    print ('Hello!')
```
Make an indent here.

= a repeat loop, saying 'Hello' 10 times.

4
```
from time import sleep
sleep (5)
```
= wait 5 seconds

5
```
player_1 = 0
```
= set a variable (player_1) to 0

6
```
player 1 = player 1 + 1
```
= increasing a variable's number by 1

7
```
==
```
= 'equals' to an operator (remember how operators are used in Scratch, with green operator blocks?)

8

```
<
```

= 'less than' an operator

9

```
>
```

= 'more than' an operator

10

```
<=
```

= less than or equal to an operator

11

```
>=
```

= more than or equal to an operator

12

Press 'enter' on your keyboard after this line.

```
from random import randint
randint(1,1000)
```

Press enter after this line and Python selects a random number between 1 to 1,000. The numbers can be changed.

= Adding the random function.

TOP TIP

The F5 button is a shortcut for the 'run' command. While you're in the code window, click it to run your script.

13

```
from turtle import *
```

= gives access to the turtle commands and controls. Python's turtle is a system that lets you draw.

14

```
a='Please'
b='feed'
c='me!'
print(a,b,c)
```

a, b, c can be any words you like.

= adding three variables together. When typed into the shell, this creates the output 'Please feed me!'

> NUMBER CRUNCH

Advanced Python code can be used to work out big calculations and solve number problems. Lots of companies use it to calculate equations and sums. Here you'll learn the basics of how it can add, multiply, divide and subtract.

Do the coding and calculations below in the **shell window.** Open up IDLE on your computer and a screen like this should appear. Type these numbers after the **'>>>'** and press 'enter' to find the output **(answer).**

```
>>> 12345 + 567654
579999
```
Answer!

Your keyboard's usual '-' button will carry out subtractions. The '/' and '*' buttons needs to be used for dividing and multiplying sums. Have a go at using all four and you'll see how quickly Python generates the answer.

- = subtraction
/ = division
* = multiplication

This piece of Python code, in the shell window, also completes addition commands. It differs from what we see on a calculator screen, because it types out the whole sum.

```
>>> num1 = 1.5
>>> num2 = 6
>>> sum = float(num1) + float(num2)
>>>> print('The sum of {0} and {1} is {2}'.
format(num1, num2, sum))
The sum of 1.5 and 6 is 7.5
```
Press 'enter' after this part.

Use brackets in your maths Python code, just like here, and it will work out
the sum in the bracket, then carry out the rest of the command.

```
>>> (10 / 10) * 10
10.0
```

```
>>> 345 * (2 + 2)
1380
```

Here's an example of how Python does clever maths, plus stuff that Scratch
can't match! Enter this code in the sheil window. It calculates the square root of 9,
16 and 100. The square root of a number is a number multiplied by itself to equal
a certain other number. So the square root of 9 is 3, because 3 x 3 equals 9.

```
>>> import math
>>> value1 = 9
>>> value2 = 16
>>> value3 = 100
>>>
>>> print(math.sqrt(value1))
3.0
>>> print(math.sqrt(value2))
4.0
>>> print(math.sqrt(value3))
10.00
```

This gives you access to the math
commands in Python.

Press 'enter' here to find the
output of each value.

Numbers are
EVERYWHERE
so the more
we understand
them, the better!

> GO TO THE LIBRARY

Python code can be taken from pre-existing packs, called libraries. This saves you time having to write new code. This book has already revealed some, like the turtle and math libraries, and here are other common libraries and what they offer.

>>> PYGAME

This is an exciting module that helps to write computer gaming code. It opens the door to cool graphics, sounds and other effects.

>>> TIME

As well as giving the date and time, this module can tell you random things, such as what day it will be 267 days from now. 'Datetime' and 'calendar' are similar modules.

>>> TKINTER

Advanced programmers make use of the tkinter module to help them link users with other programs.

>>> SOCKET

The socket module works to allow computers to link together in a network and through the internet. It helps website browsing by using a 'server' and a 'client'.

>>> MAILBOX

This module, and classes within it, help programmers to access email mailboxes and messages they contain.

>>> WXPYTHON

A type of Graphical User Interface (GUI) that helps Python programmers add widgets. Widgets can be things like textboxes and images.

>>> WINSOUND

If you use a Windows PC, winsound can give you access to a range of basic sounds, such as a simple 'beep' noise.

>>> CSV

Meaning 'Comma Separated Values', CSV is a popular module when working with spreadsheets and databases in Excel.

```
>>> import time
```

To make use of the commands in a library, just type 'import' and the name of the library at the start of your code in the code window.

LIBRARY CHECKLIST

Tick the libraries you've used, then write your favourite thing about each one!

☐ **Pygame**

☐ **Time**

☐ **Tkinter**

☐ **Socket**

☐ **Mailbox**

☐ **Wxpython**

☐ **Winsound**

☐ **CSV**

> VARIABLES AND STRINGS

These are two important parts when creating code in Python. Variables and strings are different data that make up instructions in your script. Numbers and Booleans (a value that's true or false) are examples of other data.

>>> STRINGS

If you have a list of characters in a particular order in the code in your window, this is a string. Characters can be letters, numbers, punctuation or symbols - anything you can type on your keyboard. Strings can be placed inside single or double quote marks, but use the same (single or double) throughout. It can be neater to use single quote marks, though.

The simple exercise you did on page 60, when you wrote your first Python code, was a string. Here's another to try in the shell window:

```
>>> a = 'What time is it?'
>>> b = 'The time is nearly 5.30pm!'
>>> c = 'The match starts at 5.30pm. Time to go!'
>>> d = a + b + c
>>> print(d)

What time is it? The time is nearly 5.30pm!
The match starts at 5.30pm.
Time to go!
```

This is an example of adding strings together to create an output. The three strings of a, b and c are added together to form the variable 'd'.

>>> STRING TIP

Don't use an apostrophe when writing a string. Python will think it's a command - the same as a single quote mark ('). Instead use the '\' symbol before the apostrophe to signify this.

Python can tell you what type of data you have in your code. Carrying on from the above example, write this and press 'enter':

```
>>> a = 'What time is it?'
>>> b = 'The time is nearly 5.30pm!'
>>> c = 'The match starts at 5.30pm. Time to go!'
>>> d = a + b + c
>>> print(d)
What time is it? The time is nearly 5.30pm! The match starts at 5.30pm.
Time to go!

>>> type('a')
<class 'str'>
```

The 'class 'str' shows the data is a string.

Type the 'type' command, followed by whatever data you have used, which is 'a' in this case.

>>> VARIABLES

In Python, a variable is a place where information for text or a number can be named and stored (remembered). A string can be placed in a variable and given a value. A variable must be followed by the equals (=) sign on the keyboard, then the value of that variable.

```
>>> length = 5
>>> width = 10
>>> area = length * width
>>> print('The area is', area)
The area is 50
```

This string is given a variable 5.

This string has a variable of 10.

Telling Python to reveal what the area size is.

Inform that to work out the area, length must be multiplied by width.

GUESS THE NUMBER GAME

Here's a longer piece of Python code to try out. It may look confusing, but when it's broken down, it will make sense! At the end you'll be able to play a Python game where you have a certain number of attempts to guess a random number. Good luck!

```python
import random
guessesTaken = 0
print('Hello')
number = random.randint(1, 10)
print('I am thinking of a number between 1 and 10')
while guessesTaken < 3:
    print('Take a guess')
    guess = input()
    guess = int(guess)
    guessesTaken = guessesTaken + 1
    if guess < number:
        print('Your guess is too low')
    if guess > number:
        print('Your guess is too high')
    if guess == number:
        break
if guess == number:
    guessesTaken = str(guessesTaken)
    print('Good job! You guessed the number in ' + guessesTaken + '
guesses!')
if guess !=number:
    number = str(number)
    print('No. The number I was thinking of was ' + number)
```

There must be four spaces in front of 'print' here, and for the next four lines.

HASHTAG HELP

Programmers often add helpful notes and explanations in their Python code, beginning with the hashtag (#) key. It can let other programmers who are using the code know what to do in certain places. For example, at the very start of this code you could write '# Have a go at this fun random number game!' Python ignores everything that goes after the '#' sign on that line and won't try to read it as code.

```
if guess !=number:
    number = str(number)
    print('No. The number I was thinking of was ' + number)
#Guess the Number Game. Have fun coding!
```

Open IDLE on your computer. This code needs to be written in the shell window. Then go to 'File' and 'New File'. Go to 'Save As' and name the file 'GuessNumber'. Remember that if you don't save at the start, you run the risk of losing any code you create if your computer crashes. Saving also means that you can run the code in sections as you work through it, just to make sure it's working okay.

TOP TIP

Type everything very carefully. Copy all lower and upper case letters correctly, quotes marks, colons and so on. If you get a red error message when you run the code, this is usually because of a spelling mistake.

Leave a total of 8 spaces before 'print' here.

When you have finished, save again. Then go to 'run' and 'run module' and you should be able to play the game.

The next page explains the number game!

> GUESS THE NUMBER GAME EXPLAINED

Well done for making the game on the previous page work! It probably took you a while to type out the code, but the more you practise with Python, the more confident you'll become.

When you run the program, it should look a bit like this...

```
Hello!
I am thinking of a number between 1 and 10
Take a guess
4
Your guess is too low
Take a guess
5
Your guess is too low
Take a guess
6
Good job! You guessed my number in 3 guesses!
```

Now go through the Python code, step by step, and get more information on what some of the lines of code mean.

```
import random
```

= This is an import statement, bringing the 'random' module into your program.

```
guessesTaken = 0
```

=   Sets a new variable, called guessesTaken. The number of guesses the player has made is stored in this variable. At this point the player hasn't made any guesses, so the number (called an 'integer') is 0.

```
print('Hello')
```

=   The first thing your Python code says.

```
number = random.randint(1, 10)
```

=   An instruction to call in the function 'randint'. The random value of the number you have to guess is between '1 and 10', because of your instruction here. You could change this to any two values - 1 to 1,000, for example - which will make the game harder.

```
print('I am thinking of a number between 1 and 10')
```

=   Now you are broadcasting a message in your code, to come after the first 'Hello!'. You are telling the player that you are thinking of a number between the two values in the previous line of code.

```
while guessesTaken < 3:
```

=   This is called a 'while statement'. It has two values - the value in the variable 'guessesTaken' and the integer value of 3. These are connected by a comparison operator, the 'less than' < sign. This line of code works like a 'true or false' statement.

```
    print('Take a guess')
    guess = input()
```

=   Here you're allowing the player to type their first guess at the random number. The number becomes stored as a variable called 'guess'.

```
    guess = int(guess)
```

=   Calls in a function. 'int()' takes one argument and turns it into an integer value.

```
    guessesTaken = guessesTaken + 1
```

=   This acts as a loop, where each time a guess is taken,
the number of guesses is incremented by 1.

```
    if guess < number:
        print('Your guess is too low')
    if guess > number:
        print('Your guess is too high')
```

=   An 'if' statement. Here, the player's guess is checked to see if it is less than
the secret number.

```
    if guess == number:
        break
```

=   A 'break' statement checks if the guess number is equal to the actual number.

```
  if guess == number:
     guessesTaken = str(guessesTaken)
     print('Good job! You guessed the number in ' + guessesTaken + ' guesses!')
```

=   These lines are executed if the 'if statement' in the previous code is true. The string
function displays the number of guesses taken by the player.

```
  if guess !=number:
     number = str(number)
     print('No. The number I was thinking of was ' + number)
```

=   '!=' means a 'not equal to' comparison operator. It checks if the player's last guess was
not equal to the secret number. The code then reveals what the number was.

Use this space to scribble your workings out, make notes, or just plan your next project!

> CODING QUIZ!

Time for a quick test of your coding skills and powers. All of the questions are about Scratch and Python, which you've read in this book. Good luck cracking the code!

1 What do the initials MIT mean?

A. Michigan International Technology

B. Massachusetts Institute of Technology

C. Mission Impossible Today

2 The Scratch homepage is known as the...

A. Interface

B. Integer

C. Palette

3 To change the appearance of a sprite, which tab do you need to click first?

A. File

B. Sounds

C. Costumes

4 What colour are Scratch 'sensing' blocks?

A. Pink

B. Yellow

C. Blue

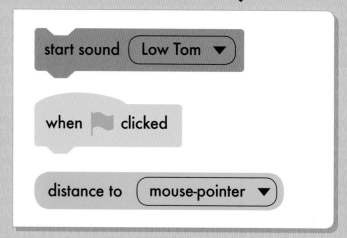

5 The horizontal and vertical positions in Scratch are known by which two letters?

A. X and X

B. Y and U

C. X and Y

6 The 'forever' and 'repeat' are known as what type of blocks?

A. Loop

B. Project

C. Run

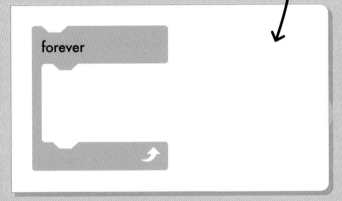

7 In Python, what two types of window are used?

A. Strings and values

B. Code and shell

C. Variable and broadcast

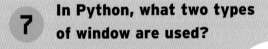

8 To make an instruction appear when you run something in Python, what do you first need to type?

A. return

B. print

C. import

9 If you edit another Scratcher's project, what is this called?

A. Remixing

B. Scratching

C. Messing

10 What type of Scratch block is this?

A. Tutorial

B. Operators

C. Motion

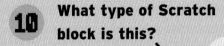

> CODING GLOSSARY

Backdrop

The name given to the background in Scratch. Sprites appear on the backdrop, which can be selected from the backdrop library.

Backpack

A time-saving storage device which Scratch scripts and sprites can be dragged to and then quickly accessed again for other projects.

Block

Scratch code is built using simple colour-coded blocks that already exist.

Costume

A sprite's appearance can be edited in the costumes tab.

Extension

From the interface, extensions can be selected such as music, video sensing and text to speech.

IDLE

Meaning Integrated Development and Learning Environment. Opening IDLE in Python allows a programmer to write code.

Interface

The general homepage for Scratch, where projects begin and information and instructions can be selected.

My Stuff

The area of Scratch where a user's projects are stored and where projects can be shared with others.

Offline

When a Scratch user is operating a computer that is not connected to the internet.

Online

If a Scratch user is online he or she is connected to a computer that has internet access enabled.

Palette

Scratch coding blocks are dragged from the palette on the left of the screen, to the scripting area.

Print

In Python, the 'print' command is an instruction to write text on the screen.

Programmer

A person who gives instructions to a computer by creating code for it to follow.

Project

Programs made in Scratch are called projects. These include games, animations, videos and music.

Scratcher

Term used to describe a person who uses Scratch.

Script

In Scratch, a script is a list or set of blocks that give instructions.

Shell and code windows

The two types of windows that will display when using Python.

Sprite

Images in Scratch that can be instructed to make movements and sounds, play games and do many other things. They are stored in the sprite library.

Stage

On the right of the interface. The stage is where code is run once a script is completed.

Upload

In Scratch, personalized sprites, backdrops and costumes can be added to a project by uploading them.

Variable

Used in Python and Scratch. A place where changeable information can be stored.

> INDEX